Bullying Prevention and Intervention

The Guilford Practical Intervention in the Schools Series

Kenneth W. Merrell, Series Editor

Books in this series address the complex academic, behavioral, and social–emotional needs of children and youth at risk. School-based practitioners are provided with practical, research-based, and readily applicable tools to support students and team successfully with teachers, families, and administrators. Each volume is designed to be used directly and frequently in planning and delivering educational and mental health services. Features include lay-flat binding to facilitate photocopying, step-by-step instructions for assessment and intervention, and helpful, timesaving reproducibles.

Recent Volumes

Assessing Culturally and Linguistically Diverse Students: A Practical Guide
  Robert L. Rhodes, Salvador Hector Ochoa, and Samuel O. Ortiz

Mental Health Medications for Children: A Primer
  Ronald T. Brown, Laura Arnstein Carpenter, and Emily Simerly

Clinical Interviews for Children and Adolescents: Assessment to Intervention
  Stephanie H. McConaughy

Response to Intervention: Principles and Strategies for Effective Practice
  Rachel Brown-Chidsey and Mark W. Steege

The ABCs of CBM: A Practical Guide to Curriculum-Based Measurement
  Michelle K. Hosp, John L. Hosp, and Kenneth W. Howell

Fostering Independent Learning: Practical Strategies to Promote Student Success
  Virginia Smith Harvey and Louise A. Chickie-Wolfe

Helping Students Overcome Substance Abuse: Effective Practices for Prevention and Intervention
  Jason J. Burrow-Sanchez and Leanne S. Hawken

School-Based Behavioral Assessment: Informing Intervention and Instruction
  Sandra Chafouleas, T. Chris Riley-Tillman, and George Sugai

Collaborating with Parents for Early School Success: The Achieving–Behaving–Caring Program
  Stephanie H. McConaughy, Pam Kay, Julie A. Welkowitz, Kim Hewitt, and Martha D. Fitzgerald

Helping Students Overcome Depression and Anxiety, Second Edition:
A Practical Guide
  Kenneth W. Merrell

Inclusive Assessment and Accountability: A Guide to Accommodations
for Students with Diverse Needs
  Sara E. Bolt and Andrew T. Roach

Bullying Prevention and Intervention: Realistic Strategies for Schools
  Susan M. Swearer, Dorothy L. Espelage, and Scott A. Napolitano

Bullying Prevention and Intervention

Realistic Strategies for Schools

SUSAN M. SWEARER
DOROTHY L. ESPELAGE
SCOTT A. NAPOLITANO

THE GUILFORD PRESS
New York   London

© 2009 The Guilford Press
A Division of Guilford Publications, Inc.
72 Spring Street, New York, NY 10012
www.guilford.com

Printed in Canada

This book is printed on acid-free paper.

Last digit is print number: 9 8 7 6 5 4 3 2 1

Library of Congress Cataloging-in-Publication Data

Swearer, Susan M.
  Bullying prevention and intervention : realistic strategies for schools / Susan M. Swearer,
Dorothy L. Espelage, Scott A. Napolitano.
     p. cm. — (Guilford practical intervention in the schools series)
  Includes bibliographical references and index.
  ISBN 978-1-60623-021-3 (pbk. : alk. paper)
    1. Bullying in schools—United States—Prevention.   2. Bullying in schools—United States—
Psychological aspects.   I. Espelage, Dorothy L. (Dorothy Lynn)   II. Napolitano, Scott A.   III.
Title.
  LB3013.32.S94 2009
  371.5′8—dc22

                                                                        2008042358

*In memory of Jessica Kassandra Haffer (www.jessicahaffer.com),
whose legacy reminds us why we must all
work compassionately and collectively to end bullying
and victimization in our schools and communities*

About the Authors

Susan M. Swearer, PhD, is Associate Professor of School Psychology at the University of Nebraska–Lincoln, Codirector of the Bullying Research Network (*http://brnet.unl.edu*), and Codirector of the Nebraska Internship Consortium in Professional Psychology. She earned her PhD in School Psychology from the University of Texas at Austin in 1997. Dr. Swearer has conducted research on the connection between mental health and bullying for over a decade.

Dorothy L. Espelage, PhD, is Professor of Child Development and Associate Chair in the Department of Educational Psychology at the University of Illinois at Urbana–Champaign. She was recently named University Scholar and has Fellow status in Division 17 (Counseling Psychology) of the American Psychological Association. Dr. Espelage earned her PhD in Counseling Psychology from Indiana University in 1997 and has conducted research on bullying for the last 15 years.

Scott A. Napolitano, PhD, is a pediatric neuropsychologist and licensed psychologist in private practice in Lincoln, Nebraska. He earned his PhD in School Psychology from the University of Texas at Austin, and completed his predoctoral internship training at the University of Nebraska Medical Center and a postdoctoral fellowship in neuropsychology at the University of Texas Southwestern Medical School. Dr. Napolitano routinely works with parents and school personnel to help students involved in bullying behaviors.

Preface

He will have to learn, I know, that all people are not just—that all men
and women are not true. Teach him that for every scoundrel there is
a hero; that for every enemy there is a friend. Let him learn early that
the bullies are the easiest people to lick.

—ABRAHAM LINCOLN

This quote from Abraham Lincoln reminds us that bullying is an age-old problem and challenges us to be heroes and friends. We can, collectively, "lick" bullying/victimization behavior among our nation's youth. Just *how* we will reduce these destructive behaviors among school-age children is the focus of this book.

Is there a need for another book about bullying? Since the late 1980s there has been a huge increase in the literature on bullying—bullying in schools; bullying that occurs among girls (i.e., relational aggression); bullying in the workplace; bullying in middle school; cyberbullying; and so on. In fact, a literature search using the key words *bully* and *bullying* revealed a 200% increase in published articles and books on bullying from 1997 to 2007. Yet, despite this huge increase in writing and research about bullying, we still don't have very good solutions about what to *do* about bullying, how to *stop* bullying, or, more realistically, how to *reduce* bullying behaviors among school-age youth.

There is a need for a book that provides a practical road map for educators, parents, and students on how to prevent bullying/victimization and how to effectively intervene when these behaviors occur. This book was written as a result of years of feedback from teachers, parents, and students who struggle with what to do about bullying. Drs. Swearer and Espelage have presented hundreds of workshops about bullying around the United States, and the uniform question asked is, "How can we stop bullying?" Dr. Napolitano works with hundreds of children, adolescents, and their families in private practice, and the uniform question that parents ask is, "What can we do about the bullying?" We've been asked this same question for over a decade, and we hope that this book provides some suggestions for how to effectively stop this pervasive phenomenon in our schools. Parents, students, educators, and researchers are collectively frustrated with trying to find solutions for bullying. Researchers who study bullying and aggression have levied theories and conducted many studies on the causes, correlates, and consequences of bullying/victimization among school-age youth. There is a lot that we know about bullying/victimization. However, there's a lot that we still don't know about these behaviors. Our collective backgrounds as researchers, educators, psychologists, and parents guide the blending of research and practice in this book in an effort to provide the reader with realistic strategies for bullying prevention and intervention. Many practical examples are drawn from our research, workshops, consultation, and practice with real people who are struggling with the real problem of what to do about bullying in our schools and communities. All the case examples in this book are a compilation of stories from our experiences or are stories that are in the public domain. With the exception of the case of Jessii Haffer in Chapter 5, the children's names are pseudonyms. All of the "Draw a Bully" pictures appearing throughout the text were drawn by real children in our work with students across the United States. Our goal is to present to you a book that illustrates the complexity of bullying behaviors and to provide suggestions for real strategies to prevent and reduce bullying in your schools, homes, and communities.

OUTLINE OF THE BOOK

Despite the glaring chasm between research and practice noted above, much of the extant psychological literature on bullying and victimization often fails to translate findings into guidelines for practice. However, we believe that school administrators, teachers, and parents can utilize research findings on youth bullying, aggression, and violence to determine which course of action to take to effectively reduce bullying in their schools and communities.

Although there are many bullying prevention and intervention programs on "the market," we do not discuss or recommend any existing programs in this book. Instead, we provide a decision-making rubric for selecting prevention and intervention strategies to reduce bullying. Given the number of programs designed to reduce bullying in schools, it is beyond the scope of this book to address each program's strengths and weaknesses. Thus, this book is a road map that provides realistic suggestions and ideas that educators, parents, and students can use to reduce bullying in their schools.

Nine chapters comprise this road map for navigating bullying/victimization prevention and intervention. Chapter 1, "Bullying Behaviors in Elementary, Middle, and High Schools," sets the stage for our understanding of bullying across the school years. Bullying/victimization is defined, and some of the research on bullying across elementary, middle, and high schools is briefly reviewed. Chapter 2, "Social-Ecological Problems Associated with Bullying Behaviors," reviews the individual, peer group, school, family, community, and societal correlates and consequences of involvement in bullying/victimization. It is clear that the social ecology in which all humans function interacts in a complex dynamic, which either perpetuates or inhibits bullying behaviors. Chapter 3, "Understanding Bullying as a Social Relationship Problem," describes what we know about the social conditions that support bullying behaviors and frames the problem of bullying as a breakdown of social relationships. When relationships are broken and are not nurtured, negative consequences such as bullying and litigation about bullying behaviors can occur. Chapter 4, "Developing and Implementing an Effective Anti-Bullying Policy," provides realistic strategies for policy development and implementation in schools. Relatedly, Chapter 5, "Legal Issues for School Personnel," reviews state laws and statutes on bullying and provides suggestions for dealing with the increased litigation over bullying. Chapter 6, "Using Your Own Resources to Combat Bullying," walks the reader through realistic strategies to use existing resources and structures in schools to reduce bullying among school-age youth. Chapter 7, "Practical Strategies to Reduce Bullying," reviews individual, peer group, and home–school strategies to reduce bullying. Chapter 8, "The Impact of Technology on Relationships," reviews what we know about how technology is used to bully others and provides suggestions for dealing with cyberbullying. Finally, Chapter 9, "Evaluating Your Efforts," provides suggestions, using a real example of data-based decision making, for evaluating your efforts to reduce bullying/victimization. Each chapter provides a case study that illustrates the principles in the chapter and a series of questions to help the reader think through some of the complex issues raised in each chapter. Collectively, we hope to stimulate creative thinking and help create realistic strategies for preventing and "licking" bullying in our schools.

Acknowledgments

We are very grateful to all the students, clients, parents, teachers, school administrators, graduate students, and colleagues who have given their time, stories, and dedication to understanding the causes, correlates, and nature of bullying behaviors. We thank the thousands of students over the years who have drawn pictures of bullying, who have participated in focus groups about bullying, and who have helped advance our research in real-world ways. We have become better researchers and clinicians as a result of these important interactions.

We owe a great deal of gratitude to Mr. Patrick Decker, principal of Maxey Elementary School in Lincoln, Nebraska, and to the wonderful Maxey third-grade team (Dr. Carmen Zalman, Ms. Carole Glenn, Mr. Dwight Thiemann, Ms. Ann Hagaman, and Ms. Pam Siefert) and the 2006–2007 third-grade students who participated in the Bullying Literature Project, which is described in Chapter 6.

Susan M. Swearer would like to acknowledge her graduate students at the University of Nebraska–Lincoln who are current members of the Target Bullying Research Project: Rhonda Turner, Amanda Siebecker, Lynae Frerichs, Jami Givens, Cixin Wang, Adam Collins, and Brandi Berry. These students all helped in various aspects of this book project. She would also like to thank her husband, Scott A. Napolitano, for his clinical perspective on the issue of bullying/victimization and his unwavering support for this book project, and their daughters, Catherine and Alexandra, who make their lives a joy to live every day.

Dorothy L. Espelage would like to thank all her mentors and friends across the world who support her passion for her work and acknowledge all of her current and former graduate students at the University of Illinois at Urbana–Champaign who inspired her work in this area: Melissa Holt, Megan Mayberry, Paul Poteat, Michelle Birkett, Jeri Newlin, Chad Rose, John Elliott, Christine Asidao, Sarah Mebane, and Amy VanBoven.

Scott A. Napolitano would like to thank his parents, Alexander and Virginia Napolitano, for their lifelong encouragement and support. He would also like to thank his wife, Susan, and their children, Catherine and Alexandra, for making every day an exciting adventure. Most of all, he would like to acknowledge all of the brave children and adolescents whose collective stories have inspired this project.

Contents

List of Figures, Tables, and Appendices

FIGURES

TABLES

APPENDICES

Bullying Prevention and Intervention

1

Bullying Behaviors in Elementary, Middle, and High Schools

Before we jump into the research and literature on bullying/victimization behaviors, we want to define the terminology we use throughout this book. There is convincing evidence that students do not remain "fixed" in the dichotomous roles of "bully" and "victim." In fact, these labels have proven to be problematic in the search for effective bullying prevention and intervention. Too often, adults and students want to punish the bullies or blame the victims. The mind-set of "Once a bully, always a bully" or "Once a victim, always a victim" only serves to keep us stuck in thinking that these are fixed traits in individuals. We know that many students, in fact, move in and out of these roles. When we tracked students over 3 years of middle school, we found that less that 13% remained in their initial group (whether as a bully, bully-victim, or victim; Swearer, Cary, & Frazier-Koontz, 2001). Thus, 87% of our sample changed their bullying/victimization roles during their 3 years of middle school. Indeed, an important resource on bullying prevention and intervention, *Let's Get Real* (Respect for All Project, 2004), uses a "four-square model" (see Figure 1.1) to illustrate that it is commonplace for students to move among the roles of bully, victim, bully-victim, and bystander. We do not want to perpetuate the stereotype that some students should be labeled "bullies" and some as "victims." We feel this communicates that these behaviors are unchangeable and these terms oversimplify the complexity of the bullying dynamic. Therefore, we use the term *bullying/victimization* throughout this book to communicate this dynamic interplay, and we use the term *bully-victim* to talk about the students who both bully others and who are victimized themselves. We also use the terms *students who bully* or *students who are victimized* to communicate that these are not fixed characteristics or traits in individuals and that all individuals have the capability to engage in bullying/victimization behaviors. If we want to truly reduce or stop bullying in our schools, we have to believe that these behaviors can be changed.

1

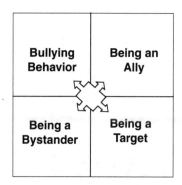

FIGURE 1.1. Four-square relational model. Reprinted by permission from the Respect for All Project.

DEFINITION OF BULLYING

The definition of bullying has been debated in the research literature, and many view bullying as a subset of aggressive behavior (Espelage, Bosworth, & Simon, 2000; Pellegrini, 2002a; Pellegrini & Long, 2002; Smith et al., 1999, 2002). Dodge and Coie (1987) define bullying as a form of proactive aggression, in which the bully is unprovoked and initiates the bullying behaviors. Olweus, Limber, and Mihalic's (1999) definition of bullying states that bullying is "aggressive behavior." However, to differentiate bullying from aggression, the bullying behavior includes an imbalance of power between the perpetrator and the target,

is intentionally harmful, and occurs repetitively (Olweus et al., 1999). The imbalance of power means that the perpetrator of bullying is stronger in some way (e.g., more popular, physically bigger, smarter, high social status) than the target. In addition to aggressive behavior, bullying includes other forms of aggression that cannot be readily observed. For example, bullying may include one person making threats to another without actually being physically aggressive. Bullying can also be perpetrated via computer or cell phone (i.e., cyberbullying) and may include relational (Crick & Grotpeter, 1995) and social (Underwood, 2003) aggression. Thus, the use of either observable or nonobservable aggressive behavior, the imbalance of power, and the repetitive nature of bullying differentiates bullying behaviors from other forms of aggression. According to the dictionary of the American Psychological Association, bullying is "persistent

threatening and aggressive behavior directed toward other people, especially those who are smaller or weaker" (VandenBos, 2007, p. 139).

ELEMENTARY SCHOOL BULLYING

Elementary school students are clearly not immune to bullying. Consider the following story: A group of kindergarten girls on the playground defined their "cool" group by wearing and trading flip-flops. They would exclude other girls by not letting them exchange the flip-flops. This relational bullying was undetected by teachers and playground aides because it was impossible for the adults to notice the type of shoes each student was wearing. The school staff only learned of the playground bullying because one of the students told her mother about it. Thus, when we are asked the question, "When does bullying start?" the answer is clearly, "By kindergarten" (Moeller, 2001).

Research has found that as many as 33.7% of U.S. elementary school students reported being frequently bullied at school (Bradshaw, Sawyer, & O'Brennan, 2007). Kochenderfer and Ladd (1996b) found that approximately 20% of kindergarteners reported being frequently victimized. Elementary students involved in bullying/victimization are not fixed in the roles of "bully" or "victim." Rather, moving in and out of these roles (i.e., bullies to victims to bully-victims) appears to be the norm (Dempsey, Fireman, & Wang, 2006). However, despite the lack of fixed roles, we do know that students who are aggressive in elementary school tend to be the same students who are aggressive in middle and high school (Harachi et al., 2006; Huesmann, Eron, Lefkowitz, & Walder, 1984; Olweus, 1993a, 1993b, 1994).

MIDDLE SCHOOL BULLYING

Clear consensus in the research literature is that bullying/victimization peak during the middle school years. The transition from elementary to middle school has been hypothesized to be related to this increase (Nansel et al., 2001; Pellegrini & Long, 2002; Solberg, Olweus, & Endresen, 2007), as students are typically negotiating new peer groups during this time. In a study of 15,686 6th- through 10th-grade students, researchers found that

29.9% of students reported moderate to frequent involvement in bullying. Of those students, 13% stated they bullied others, 10.6% reported being frequently victimized, and 6.3% endorsed both bullying/victimization (Nansel et al., 2001). Research over the past decade suggests that, among U.S. middle school students, approximately 7.5–13% bullied others; 10.6–20.7% were victimized; and 1–13% engaged in both bullying/victimization (Batsche & Knoff, 1994; Cunningham, 2007; Demaray & Malecki, 2003; Kauffman et al., 1998; Nansel et al., 2001; Seals & Young, 2003; Unnever, 2005; Wenxin, 2002). Based on a review of the bullying/victimization literature, it is clear that these are relatively common phenomena for middle school students.

HIGH SCHOOL BULLYING

Bullying during the high school years has received less attention in the literature than bullying during the elementary and middle school years. The research on bullying during later adolescence has been important in documenting the rise in harassment; thus, bullying/victimization takes on the form of harassment and the two are clearly linked. We know that sexual harassment is more common for females during high school than middle school (Gruber & Fineran, 2007). The American Association of University Women (AAUW; 1993, 2001) conducted two studies of sexual harassment in U.S. schools. Approximately 81% of students experienced sexual harassment during their school years, with rates increasing over time; 55% of 8th and 9th graders and 61% of 10th and 11th graders reported being sexually harassed. The AAUW study also found that females were sexually harassed more than males.

Unfortunately, teachers typically underestimate the levels of bullying/victimization in their schools. Bradshaw et al. (2007) surveyed both school personnel and students at more than 14 high schools in the Northeast, with the goal of determining how well high school teachers can predict the amount of bullying and harassment in their schools. Over 57% of school staff predicted that less than 10% of students at their school had been victimized. Only 9% of school staff correctly predicted that approximately 28% of high school students reported being victimized. Research has also found that elementary and middle school teachers predicted victimization of their students more accurately than high school teachers. Although the overall rates of bullying and victimization decrease during high school (Nansel et al., 2001), this phenomenon is confounded by sexual harassment and underestimations of the prevalence of bullying, victimization, and harassment.

BULLYING: INCREASED ATTENTION OR BIGGER PROBLEM?

Bullying, as illustrated in the Abraham Lincoln quote in the Preface, is an age-old problem. Although bullying has not necessarily increased in frequency as a behavioral problem over time, the attention given to bullying behaviors has increased. In the past two decades, there has been a proliferation of research on bullying and victimization worldwide and in the United States (Espelage et al., 2000; Espelage, Holt, & Henkel, 2003; Espelage &

Swearer, 2003; Hoover, Oliver, & Hazler, 1992; Horne, Bartolomucci, & Newman-Carlson, 2003; Juvonen & Graham, 2001; Olweus et al., 1999; Salmivalli, Lagerspetz, Bjorkqvist, Osterman, & Kaukiainen, 1996; Swearer & Doll, 2001). Since 1997 a 200% increase in publications about bullying behaviors has occurred. However, despite this increased attention given to bullying, we still observe and have data that support moderate to high levels of bullying in our nation's schools.

Much of the work on bullying in the United States has been a result of high-profile school shootings: Two thirds of the school shooters reported that they had been chronically bullied throughout their school years (Vossekuil, Fein, Reddy, Borum, & Modzeleski, 2002). Although the assertion that bullying contributes to devastating, lasting negative psychological effects is not new, the fact is that, despite this proliferation of research on bullying, little is known about how to translate this research into effective practice. School administrators and teachers are selecting and implementing anti-bullying programs with very little guidance as to how to create lasting change. Although there are innumerable curricula and psychosocial programs that address school violence and anger management, as well as bullying and harassment, very few of these programs have been systemically evaluated through rigorous, empirical investigations (Furlong, Morrison, & Greif, 2003). Given this dearth of solid outcome data, how can school administrators, teachers, and parents effectively wade through the literature on bullying and make decisions about effective interventions for their schools and communities?

Fortunately, we have moved beyond trying to argue and establish that bullying exists among school-age youth and that bullying has a lasting and detrimental negative impact on everyone involved (Espelage & Swearer, 2004). At least two decades of research on bullying has established the negative psychological, social, and societal consequences of bullying behaviors; however, less is known about how to effectively translate this knowledge into real solutions for schools.

Before we can propose real solutions for reducing bullying behaviors, several myths about bullying/victimization need to be challenged. Each myth is debunked in the following eight chapters in this book.

- **Myth 1: Bullying is an isolated, individual aggressive action.** Given the definition of bullying (intent to harm, repetition, and imbalance of power), many studies that purport to assess bullying/victimization might not actually assess for these three components. Therefore, there is a need to accurately assess bullying/victimization behaviors. Bullying is *not* an isolated, aggressive action. In fact, bullying/victimization problems are influenced by peers, families, schools, and communities (see Chapter 2). Thus, bullying is best understood from a social-ecological perspective (Espelage & Swearer, 2004).
- **Myth 2: Bullying occurs between a "bully" and a "victim."** This is seldom the case. In fact, we need to "debunk this dyadic bias" (Espelage & Swearer, 2003) and recognize that bullying is a dynamic, social relationship problem (see Chapter 3) and many youth move in and out of various roles, depending on the social-ecological conditions (e.g., aggression in the home, peer group that bullies, lack of supervision in the school setting).
- **Myth 3: Anti-bullying policies are ineffective.** The negative effects of bullying/victimization can last well into adulthood. We know that anti-harassment, discrimination, and

gun-control policies have served to increase awareness of these social issues. In our experience, if anti-bullying policies are not mandated, many school districts do not willingly develop and adopt anti-bullying policies. These policies serve to increase awareness about bullying/victimization and lay the foundation for lasting social change (see Chapter 4).

- **Myth 4: Bullying is a "normal" part of growing up.** Although we know that bullying behaviors seem to peak during the middle school years (Pellegrini, 2002a, 2002b), we also know that bullying occurs among elementary school students (Bradshaw et al., 2007) and high school students (Gruber & Fineran, 2007). Bullying is a lifespan problem that is not isolated to one developmental period. Bullying is also not a normal part of growing up, and there are legal ramifications for these behaviors (see Chapter 5).

- **Myth 5: It's impossible to stop bullying.** Bullying/victimization occur in varying degrees in most schools, but there are many schools and classrooms where bullying/victimization is rare. We know that when there is positive adult leadership in schools, positive student leadership, and healthy relationships, there is less bullying. It's not impossible to stop bullying; it just takes a coordinated, intelligent effort (see Chapter 6).

- **Myth 6: Bullying prevention and intervention are complicated and expensive.** In our work with school personnel, we often hear comments about lacking resources and not being able to purchase anti-bullying programs. We counter with the simple fact that stopping bullying is all about developing healthy social relationships. Modeling and shaping children's social relationships is *free*. If we teach everyone to treat others as they wish to be treated, then an obvious extension of this logic is that bullying would not occur. Strategies for reducing bullying don't have to be complicated and expensive (see Chapter 7).

- **Myth 7: Physical bullying is more damaging than relational or verbal bullying.** In fact, the old adage "Sticks and stones may break my bones, but words will never hurt me" is untrue. Relational, verbal, and/or social bullying can be just as damaging, or even more damaging, than physical bullying. Typically, the relational bullying is undetected by adult eyes and can continue for years without consequence. Additionally, with the proliferation of access to technology (i.e., computers, cell phones), cyberbullying has become a significant problem (see Chapter 8). The negative effects of these less overt forms of bullying can last well into adulthood.

- **Myth 8: Figuring out how to evaluate anti-bullying efforts is too complicated.** Every school has a math teacher; therefore, it is not too complicated to use math and statistics to evaluate the effects of any intervention or to survey students and school personnel about bullying/victimization. In fact, these are intellectual activities that can be easily subsumed into any curriculum such as reading (see Chapter 6) or math (see Chapter 9).

TRANSLATING RESEARCH INTO REAL SOLUTIONS

It is vital that parents, educators, and students read the research about bullying and not just rely on the news media or popular press books. There are many myths about bullying that are perpetuated by the popular press. For example, many people believe that only girls engage in relational bullying. In fact, we know that boys engage in this form of bullying also. How can parents, educators, and students use research findings to inform effective practice? We hope that this book can help move adults and students into a data-based, decision-making mentality in which we make informed, intelligent decisions about how to prevent and reduce bullying/victimization behaviors in our schools and communities. This notion of data-based decision making is critical as school service providers address legal mandates to adopt anti-bullying policies.

THE 80/20 PRINCIPLE

In addition to being a road map to reducing bullying in schools, this book has an underlying thesis borrowed from Koch's (1998) 80/20 principle. Koch writes, "In society, 20 percent of the criminals account for 80 percent of the value of all crime" (1998, p. 4). Applied to bullying behaviors, this would mean that 80% of the bullying incidences are perpetrated by 20% of the students. When we examine prevalence data for bullying (Nansel et al., 2001), the 80/20 principle seems to accurately apply to this phenomenon. Therefore, the guiding question becomes, "Under what conditions does bullying occur?" If we can alter the conditions that allow bullying to occur, then we have a chance of reducing or stopping bullying behaviors from occurring in the first place.

Related to the 80/20 principle is the notion that environmental conditions can either encourage or inhibit bullying. Thus, in order to effectively reduce bullying, we have to examine all the contexts in which children function: personal, family, peer group, school, community, and society. This social ecology provides fertile ground for the conditions under which bullying can (or cannot) occur. Intervening across all these conditions will give us the chance to alter the behavior of 20% of the individuals and thus reduce 80% of the bullying incidents to close to zero.

A SOCIAL-ECOLOGICAL FRAMEWORK FOR BULLYING/VICTIMIZATION

Children's social development is often conceptualized as emerging, being maintained, and modified as a result of a child's personality characteristics and how these characteristics interact within the larger subsystems or social contexts (e.g., peers, family, schools). This perspective has been called a social-ecological theory (Bronfenbrenner, 1977, 1979) and includes four interrelated systems: microsystem, mesosystem, exosystem, and macrosystem. The *microsystem* depicts the system with which the individual has direct contact, including parents, siblings, peers, and schools. The *mesosystem* comprises the interrelations among *microsystems,* such as an adolescent's family and peers. For example, attachment to one's parents might contribute to a willingness to take risks in establishing friendships at school. The *exosystem* depicts influences from other systems, such as parental involvement in schools. Finally, the *macrosystem* includes societal and cultural influences that impact individuals. The social-ecological framework has been extended to predictive models of bullying/victimization (Espelage & Swearer, 2004; Swearer et al., 2006). We contend that bullying/victimization does not occur in isolation and, in fact, results as a complex interaction between the individual and his or her family, peer group, school community, and societal norms (see Figure 1.2; Swearer & Espelage, 2004).

CONCLUSIONS AND RECOMMENDATIONS

In this chapter, we discussed some of the research on bullying among school-age youth and outlined a social-ecological framework for understanding the complexity of these behaviors. Clearly, bullying/victimization is a complex dynamic that spans elementary, middle, and high school. This complex dynamic is further explicated in the next chapter on social-ecological problems associated with bullying behaviors.

As mentioned in the preface, each chapter contains a case example followed by a series of questions. The complexity of the bullying/victimization dynamic from a social-ecological framework is the first case study presented next.

CASE EXAMPLE: JOE—NOT A COMPLICATED NAME, BUT A COMPLICATED CASE

Joe is an 11-year-old Caucasian male who is attending public school. He comes from a middle-class family with a diverse ethnic background. His father was born and raised in the Middle East. He married an American in 1994 after a very short courtship and moved to the United States. Joe was born after a traumatic delivery in which the umbilical cord had been wrapped around his neck, and it is believed that he suffered some type of brain injury as a result of a lack of oxygen. However, Joe recovered well after delivery and showed all the signs of being a healthy, normal infant.

By the time Joe was about 1 year old, he was displaying abnormal behavior. He was very demanding, screamed a lot, was in constant motion, and still did not sleep through the night. Things continued to get worse. By the time he was about 18 months old, he would take off his diaper and smear feces all over his crib, the walls, and himself. About 3 years later, his brother was born without complications into a family unable to handle their already out-of-control 3-year-old.

Joe's parents divorced 2 years ago, after being married for more than a decade. The boys lived with their mother, who struggled to raise them, especially Joe. No one would babysit him, and he was constantly in trouble at school.

School Background

Joe has never made it through a school year without going to the principal's office on more days than not. His parents and stepparents have never made it through the year without multiple special disciplinary meetings and phone calls from the school.

Joe sometimes cries, "I just want to have friends!" His parents say that he has been saying that for years. When adults and peers first meet Joe, they find him delightful. He is very polite and animated. The problem is he cannot maintain relationships. When he meets new

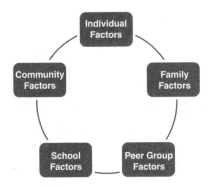

What are the factors that contribute to bullying in your school and community?

Social-Ecological Factors	Y/N?	Y/N?	Y/N?	Y/N?M	Make a list
Individual Factors	Depression?	Anxiety?	Impulsiveness?	Lack of problem solving?	Other?
Family Factors	Poor supervision?	Abuse?	Aggression in the family?	Lack of parental involvement?	Other?
Peer Group Factors	Bullying is accepted?	Bullying is done by a group of students?	Bullying is done by the athletes?	Bullying is mostly done by individuals?	Other?
School Factors	Adults bully others?	Adults don't intervene in bullying?	Students who bully are punished (versus being helped)?	The school climate is negative?	Other?
Community Factors	Are there high levels of aggression in your community?	Are there are few community resources?	Do community–school partnerships exist?	Is the school an integral part of the community?	Other?

FIGURE 1.2. Social-ecological model of bullying/victimization: Factors that contribute to bullying.

peers, they decide after a period of days or a few weeks that Joe is "weird" and that other kids think he is "weird" too. The other kids make fun of him because he is "weird." Then any child who has even considered being friends with Joe runs for the hills, and he is stuck with the rest of the outcasts and sometimes not even with *them*.

Below are some excerpts from Joe's school reports.

Third grade:

"It was evident that he has considerable difficulty with sustaining his attention to task. He tends to be very active physically, as well as impulsive and distractible, and he requires frequent redirection."

"Joe requires an inappropriate amount of personal space."

"Joe is in constant motion."

"Joe struggles in most academic areas."

"He is eager to please and enjoys being complimented on his academic successes."

"As he worked, it was noted he was very fidgety and moved around in his chair a lot. He also seemed to be scratching himself often. . . . This portion of the test was given in several parts because Joe was so itchy. It was noted that he took off his shoes during testing, yawned during his reading. . . . "

"Joe could benefit from a friendship group to help him make and maintain friends. Joe noted that having friends is something he would like."

Fourth grade:

"His behavior is such that he needs daily opportunities to learn and practice specific social skills needed in conversation, friendship, cooperation, and studying/learning."

"A consistent concern expressed by the educational staff was the difficulty Joe exhibited in his social interactions."

"Joe's teachers expressed concerns about his social capabilities and his struggle with friendship. They commented about the boy he had reported as bullying him and described their relationship as a two-way conflict. Joe was reported to say, 'I'll beat you up' and the other student said, 'Bring it on.' They said that Joe is constantly telling the other student that he can beat him up. Joe's mother said that he might want to be friends with the other student despite their differences."

" . . . Joe is bright and significantly underachieving."

"Inappropriate behavior was also identified as problematic . . . School records and reports from teachers indicate that profanity, sexual innuendoes, threats of aggression, not following teacher requests, fighting with students, outbursts of anger, stealing, and lying have occurred in school since he began attending in September."

"When asked about friends, he said that he has one friend who lives next to dad. Otherwise, he could name no friends at his current school. He named several boys with whom he wanted to be friends who he considered to be fast runners."

In May of Joe's fourth-grade year, after several incidences involving bullying and Joe bullying back, Joe's mother was asked not to bring him back to school until he was under control. His mother admitted him to the behavioral unit at a local hospital, after 1 week they pronounced him "perfectly normal" and released him with no further treatment, therapy, or direction ordered. The mother gave her ex-husband custody, and Joe came to live with his father and second wife.

Fifth grade:

"Goal #2: To improve social skills and peer relationships, Joe will demonstrate the following in at least 8 out of 10 trials."

Goal number 2 was to be taught by the school counselor, his teacher, his special education teacher, and speech language pathologist. The evaluation method was behavior observation, charting, and "oral performance." Unfortunately, Joe did not qualify for any type of formal social skills training or group settings in which he could safely "practice."

Progress report from fifth grade:

"Joe tries to follow classroom expectations, but he is not always successful."

"I am concerned about Joe's seemingly poor self-concept. This impacts how well he is able to interact with others" (and yet he was marked as having made "adequate progress" in this area). Joe's progress reports almost always marked his individualized education plan progress as "adequate" even though there were obvious problems, mostly resulting from his social skills, attention span, and low self-esteem.

After-School Program

The disciplinary report concerns an argument with other kids in the after-school program. The kids reported Joe was cheating, and he very stubbornly denied it and tried to speak badly of the supervising teacher:

" . . . I told him he had to sit next to me and we would no longer tolerate any talking bad about teachers with other kids at the after-school program. This is what leads to violence."

A few days after this incident, the final straw was drawn. Joe just couldn't help himself and continued to participate in conversations at the after-school program that were negative and included threats of violence toward the teacher. Joe had complained throughout the entire school year that the after-school teacher did not like him and that she was unfair to him and rude. The parents also believed that the teacher simply didn't like Joe. In the end, Joe and another child discussed how they could get revenge on the teacher by bringing a gun to school and shooting her. Joe was permanently banned from the after-school program. The other boy was allowed to return after a 3-day suspension.

The Parents' Thoughts and Experiences

Joe tells his stepmother that the kids use expletives when calling him a fat, stupid freak. Some days he comes home from school stressed out, angry, and depressed. Sometimes he comes home in a good mood and does not seem to care how he was treated that day. He feels that the teachers don't care about him and that they let the other kids get away with the same things that he is getting in trouble for. Joe is labeled a troublemaker, and it seems like he is always getting negative attention. His stepmother thinks that the teacher really tried in the beginning, but as the year wore on, so did her patience and workload. The other kids know how to stay out of trouble, even if they are engaging in bullying behaviors. Joe, on the other hand, does not know how to do that and is always visible on the teacher's radar. It is very easy to blame Joe.

Joe came home one day very quiet and he seemed sad. Normally he is bouncing off the wall, so the stepmother asked what had happened. He told her that he was playing basketball by himself at recess when some other kids his age came and wanted to play, but not with him. He told her that he kept shooting hoops in the same basketball hoop that he had been using. The other kids wanted to use the whole court and kept shoving him aside when they went to his basket, getting in his face and calling him names. Joe is a very stubborn child and he isn't about to back down, so he continued to try and shoot baskets. The situation escalated to shouting and pushing, and it finally gained the attention of a teacher supervising recess. According to Joe, the teacher made him go "sit at the wall" for the remainder of recess while the other boys played basketball.

On another occasion in the after-school program, Joe seemed to have finally made a friend. His friend Jack was 6 years old and got along well with Joe. It seems that younger kids tend to be more accepting of other kids because Jack didn't seem to notice Joe's unacceptable social behaviors. Joe went over to Jack's house to play with him a few times, and he told his stepmother that even though Jack was only 6, he was a very cool kid. One day when Joe went over to see whether Jack could play, Jack's mother told Joe that he couldn't come over anymore because she felt that he was too old to play with Jack. He was very disappointed.

It was family night at Dairy Queen and Joe wanted to go. He said that all of his "friends" would be there and that he had to go and he did not want his parents to go because they would embarrass him. The parents went and promised to sit in the corner and only talk to each other. They were the first ones there from their school. As the parents watched kids trickle in with their families, they observed their behaviors. When there were only a few kids, they were all very polite to each other engaging in small talk. They seemed to include Joe. Once more kids started to come, they started segregating more. All of the kids seemed to have a "place" except Joe. Being the social, excitable kid that Joe is, he was trying his best to talk to anyone who would listen. The kids turned their backs on him. Some rolled their eyes or displayed other negative, nonverbal behaviors. In the end, most of the kids had moved outside. Joe went to. He was sitting on the curb, by himself, eating his ice cream.

Joe bullies back. He is constantly looking for some form of revenge, whether it is a silly little joke that he comes up with, with that kid being the butt of the joke, or talking about some plan of violence toward that bully or silly practical jokes. One time Joe and his step-mother were at Wal-Mart. He was dressed like a soccer player. Joe does not play soccer on a team, but he likes soccer and is proud that his dad played soccer. At the store, Joe wandered alone into an aisle where some 17- and 18-year-old girls were shopping. When he returned to his stepmother, his eyes were wide and he was jittery. His stepmother asked him what was wrong. One of the girls had said something to the effect of "Look at the little soccer boy." Joe assumed that they were making fun of him. Throughout the rest of the shopping trip, Joe concocted his plan to sneak into the parking lot and place some type of a bomb on the girls' car intended to maul or fatally injure them as a punishment for making him feel bad.

At school Joe usually bullies by using threats of violence and profanity. Joe has not been known to bully an innocent target; it is always in response to being bullied or treated badly. He will rarely actually instigate any physical contact but will react to physical contact. He tells kids whom he feels are persecuting him that they are "retards" and just about anything else he can come up with whether it makes sense or not. Usually to make himself feel better and more superior in front of others, he will make up ridiculous stories like his dad was run over by a train and survived or one time he literally had his finger cut off . . . and survived. He also tells "stories" to get attention . . . any kind of attention. Joe will tell people that he drives his dad's car. He tells others that his parents allow him to watch R-rated movies and play violent video games and that he owns a gun. He tells people that he speaks Arabic (he does not), and when it suits him, he is Norwegian. He also falsely claims that his parents let him stay up all night.

His family bullies Joe too. Joe has two female cousins the same age as him. They have been tormenting, excluding, and making fun of him for years, and no one seems to do anything about it. Joe's 8-year-old brother has discovered the enjoyment of being mean to his older brother as well. He probably learned these behaviors from the cousins. One time when the cousins and another male child were spending the night, Joe's stepmother caught the other kids up in the middle of the night standing in the hallway giggling. She found that Joe's brother was showing the other kids that Joe wears Pull-Ups to bed and that his "crack" hangs out of them because he is too big for them. The cousins aren't allowed to spend the night any more.

Thoughts about Joe's Case

In conclusion, school is not a positive experience for students with the type of challenges that Joe faces. The teachers and schools simply do not have the resources or are not offering the resources needed to guide children with behavior disorders. Kids like Joe are absolute targets, and they don't have the skills necessary to deal with their anxiety, sadness, and anger. They need to be taught social skills and how to interact with peers who bully them.

Schools need to do a better job of identifying bullying behaviors and intervene. Joe is being left behind by his community, peers, doctors, counselors, psychiatrists, family members, teachers, and the entire public school system. His parents worry about Joe and they wonder what Joe will be capable of as he grows. Their greatest hope is that Joe will be strong and overcome these difficulties in spite of adversity. Their greatest fear is that he will succumb to the daily emotional attacks he endures and the literal struggle within himself.

FOLLOW-UP QUESTIONS

1. Keep in mind the social-ecological model of bullying. What are the individual factors impacting this case? Family factors? Peer group factors? School factors? Community factors? Cultural factors?

2. We know that zero-tolerance approaches are typically ineffective for these types of students. What are some alternatives that your school has used when students threaten violence? Are suspension and expulsion your only choices?

3. How would you describe this family's relationship with their son's elementary school personnel? How can you support and strengthen home–school partnerships in your school?

4. Many students in special education experience problems with bullying and/or victimization. Think of the special needs students in your school. Is the school climate supportive for these students? How does your school promote respect for differences?

2

Social-Ecological Problems
Associated with Bullying Behaviors

In Chapter 1, we outlined a social-ecological model of bullying behavior based on Bronfenbrenner's (1979) well-known social-ecological theory. In plain terms, bullying behaviors from this perspective emerges from a complex intersection of children's personality and disposition, which becomes modified as they enter into various contexts across early childhood and adolescence. For example, we are often asked by parents, colleagues, and friends, along with hairdressers and cab drivers, the all too familiar question, "What causes children to bully others?" In order to answer this question, the following scenario is one that might emerge from the research literature.

Imagine 11-year-old Sally, who has a personality that might be described as impulsive and is quick to anger, especially when she experiences frustration. This alone will not cause us concern that she might bully others. However, if Sally resides in a family in which poor anger management skills are modeled or there is a general lack of emotional regulation training and her sister bullies her, then there is more evidence that she might be at risk to bully her peers at school. Then we find out that Sally goes to a school in which there is no explicit bully policy and bullying is not addressed by teachers, staff, or administrators. Her individual personality characteristics will interact with these less-than-prosocial environments, and then when she joins a peer group in which the members bully others for fun, Sally is at risk for joining in. Within this example, it is clear that individual personality factors influence whether these social contexts exacerbate or minimize the development of bullying perpetration. Children who are victims of bullying also have individual personality characteristics (e.g., shyness, social skills deficits) that influence how their social development will progress as they enter different social contexts.

Individual and social contextual factors are embedded within one another, and they influence each other in a reciprocal and circular manner. That is, children and adolescents who bully others will inevitably be received differently in their homes, schools, and communities. Similarly, children and adolescents who are victimized will, in some cases, approach these social contexts in ways that might contribute to increased victimization across different domains, or it might lead them to not reach out to others and fully take advantage of these environments. And to be honest, children and adolescents who are victims will perceive, sometimes accurately, these environments as unsafe and intolerable. This complex dynamic is exactly the focus of this chapter. Children and adolescents who are identified as bullies, victims, or bully-victims face consequences of their experiences in their own individual social development and mental health and in their interactions with family, friends, peers, and schoolteachers and administrators. In this chapter, the research on these consequences, both good and bad, is briefly reviewed, with special attention given to the clinical implications of the research.

PSYCHOLOGICAL CORRELATES

A wide range of emotions surround experiences of being victimized or perpetrating bullying. Victimized youth report more loneliness, greater school avoidance, more suicidal ideation, and less self-esteem than their nonbullied peers (Hawker & Boulton, 2000; Kochenderfer & Ladd, 1996a). Depression also has been found to be a common mental health symptom experienced by male and female victims of bullying (Kaltiala-Heino, Rimpelae, & Rantanen, 2001; Swearer, Song, Cary, Eagle, & Mickelson, 2001). Further, being victimized is associated with physical health problems, such as headaches and stomachaches (Srabstein, McCarter, Shao, & Huang, 2006). Victims are also often characterized as more insecure, anxious, and quiet than their peers (Olweus, 1995a), and children who report high rates of victimization receive lower grades than those not identified as bullies or victims (Graham, Bellmore, & Mize, 2006). Schwartz, Gorman, Nakamoto, and Toblin (2005) found that victimization predicted poor academic performance over time. Victimization impacts children both in the short term and into their adult years. Long-term impact was noted with Olweus's (1995b) longitudinal study of 23-year-old participants; those who were victimized in their youth reported greater symptoms of depression and less self-esteem than cohort peers who were not victimized.

Whereas victimized youth tend to report more internalizing behaviors (e.g., depression, anxiety), students who bully are more likely than their peers to engage in externalizing behaviors such as conduct problems, to report lower levels of school belonging, and to engage in delinquent behavior (Espelage & Holt, 2001; Haynie, Nansel, & Eitel, 2001). It appears that physical health problems are not unique to victims; that is, bullies also report more significant physical health symptoms than uninvolved youth (Srabstein et al., 2006). In addition, anger has been found to be a significant predictor of bullying perpetration (Espelage & Holt, 2001). These studies find that students who are prone to depression, and therefore have lowered self-esteem, might tease or bully others in order to make themselves feel better. This anger, if not attended to, can result in more serious criminal involvement. Olweus (1993a, 1993b) found that bullies at a young age in Norway were more likely to be convicted of crimes in adulthood, and another study of American youth identified as bullies in school found that these individuals had a 1 in 4 chance of having a criminal record by age 30 (Eron, Huesmann, Dubow, Romanoff, & Yarnel, 1987).

What is important to remember is that the majority of work relating bullying perpetration or victimization to these outcomes is largely correlational, which does not mean that perpetration or victimization *causes* these outcomes. Victimization and perpetration have been found to have complex relations with other potentially intervening or mediating variables. For example, when students are teased, for some, the teasing results in them questioning their own identity, wondering what it is about them that contributes to their victimization, and these thoughts could then lead to distressing feelings, such as depression or lowered self-confidence or self-esteem (Graham & Juvonen, 2001). It is not surprising that those students who are often victimized at school report higher levels of state and trait anxiety (Craig, 1998; Rigby & Slee, 1993). Their victimization is often unpredictable and happens in places where there are few adults, which can create fear and hypervigilance, fueling the anxiety.

Finally, it is important to recognize that bully-victims represent the most at-risk group of youth. Bully-victims are those students who report being victimized by their peers and also being perpetrators. Bully-victims demonstrate more externalizing behaviors, are more hyperactive, and have a greater probability of being referred for psychiatric consultation than their peers (Nansel et al., 2001; Nansel, Haynie, & Simons-Morton, 2003). Bully-victims have also been found to report higher levels of depression compared with both bullies and victims (Austin & Joseph, 1996; Swearer et al., 2001c). Similarly, bully-victims have been found to have lower grades than both bullies and victims and were reported by teachers to be the least engaged of their students (Graham et al., 2006).

In summary, there is considerable evidence that involvement in bullying, as a victim, bully, or bully-victim, is associated with serious short-term and long-term psychological and academic consequences. Despite this level of evidence, many children who suffer from mental and physical health symptoms go unnoticed by parents, teachers, and family physicians. It is important to notice any systematic changes in a child's or adolescent's mood or academic performance. Professionals who have any exposure to children, including nurses, social workers, teachers, and pediatricians, should specifically ask about victimization or bullying experiences. Questions should be open ended in format and should be asked in a way to normalize the experiences and to create the conditions under which students feel free to openly express their feelings.

PEER INFLUENCES

Peers play an integral role in the social development of children and adolescents. Emerging research has also shown that peers are integral in supporting and maintaining bullying victimization and perpetration in our schools. There are several dominant theories that have demonstrated that kids learn to bully each other from their peers. Additionally, some students who are bullies are among the most popular students and are looked up to by others. Although the processes of peer influence are complicated, the major theories are outlined in simple terms here to make direct points about how peers can be used to prevent bullying perpetration and victimization.

The first theory is called *homophily* (Cairns & Cairns, 1994; Espelage, Holt, & Henkel, 2003). Although the word might not be familiar to many readers, the concept behind it is simple. Take, for example, the phrase "Birds of a feather flock together." Students in late elementary school through high school tend to hang out or befriend peers who are similar to them in attitudes, interests, and behaviors. It is true that some students select each other based on similarity in these characteristics, but it is also true that peers socialize one another into acting and behaving a certain way by internalizing norms of the group (Kandel, 1978). Support for the homophily hypothesis has been documented in the bullying literature, which has found that individuals within the same friendship group tend to report engaging in similar levels of bullying behaviors (Espelage et al., 2003; Espelage, Green, & Wasserman, 2007). Put simply, bullies hang out with bullies. But not all peer groups are made up of members who perpetrate bullying from the outset. That is, bullies within a peer group with high social status socialize their friends to engage in bullying behaviors. Moreover, bullying levels within the peer group are predictive of adolescents' bullying behavior over time, even after controlling for individuals' own baseline levels of bullying, a finding that holds true for both males and females.

As seen in Figure 1.1, individuals move in and out of bullying/victimization roles. Salmivalli et al. (1996) have spent the last decade examining specifically the various roles that children play as bullying occurs. They consistently find that individuals are not victimized by a single individual. Rather, bullying involves both active and passive participation of multiple individuals. Students have been found to assist in the process by chasing or holding down the victim for the bully. Students may also reinforce bullying by encouraging the bullies to continue their aggressive behavior toward the victim or by further teasing the victim. Some students, albeit a small number, support the victimized individual by attempting to stop the bully, finding help for the victim, or providing psychological support for the victim after the bullying episode is over. Finally, other students might be classified as outsiders or bystanders; these individuals are not involved in bullying episodes, or they are those individuals who leave the situation when the bullying episode begins (Salmivalli et al., 1996).

Homophily provides some notion that children hang out with similarly minded individuals in relation to bullying. Others theories offer some explanation as to how and why this socialization occurs. Dominance theory is one of these. Aggression has long been recognized as a means of establishing dominance among children's groups. Developmental psychologists have demonstrated that establishing higher status with groups yields greater access to resources and greater control or influence over other peers (Bjorklund & Pellegrini, 2002; Boulton, 1992; Pellegrini & Long, 2002). Dominance status can be attained through either affiliative (e.g., leadership) or antagonistic (e.g., bullying) methods (Hawley, 1999). Research suggests that dominance is initially established through antagonistic methods late in elementary school, followed by affiliative methods later in middle school or further into the establishment of the peer group (Pellegrini & Long, 2002).

The need for dominance and developmental timing has offered some perspective on why the prevalence of bullying shifts over the school years. More specifically, bullying perpetration typically increases during transition periods, such as from elementary school to middle school (Pellegrini & Bartini, 2001; Pellegrini & Long, 2002). These transitions often require a change in primary affiliation groups and a new school environment. Bullying is often used at these time points to establish control over other students and directly impacts the roles that children and adolescents assume with these peer groups. An example of this phenomenon is illustrated in the following story. Data from a school district indicated that bullying behaviors in its school system dramatically increased from fifth grade (last year of elementary school) to sixth grade (first year of middle school). The elementary and the middle school staff and the district staff decided to keep the fifth-grade teams the same as the students entered sixth grade. Over time, they noted that this consistency in peer group structure between the last year of elementary school and the first year of middle school resulted in less bullying behaviors during the sixth-grade year. Additionally, the middle schools decided to have the school counselors follow the same cohort of students throughout their middle school years (versus having sixth-grade counselors, seventh-grade counselors, and eighth-grade counselors who were different across the years). This consistency in counselors for the students also helped them navigate the social intricacies of the middle school years. The collaboration between the elementary, middle, and district staff helped mitigate the dominance factor that has been associated with increases in bullying behaviors.

A third theory that is particularly relevant to understanding how peers influence and maintain bullying perpetration in our schools is attraction theory. Attraction theory posits that young adolescents become attracted to other youth who possess characteristics reflecting independence (e.g., delinquency, aggression, disobedience) and are less attracted to those who possess characteristics more descriptive of childhood (e.g., compliance, obedience) as they attempt to establish independence from their own parents (Bukowski, Sippola, & Newcomb, 2000; Moffitt, 1993). These authors argue that young adolescents manage the transition from primary to secondary schools through their attractions to peers who are aggressive. In a study of 217 boys and girls during this transition, Bukowski and colleagues found that girls' and boys' attraction to aggressive peers increased on entry to middle school. This increase was larger for girls, which is consistent with Pellegrini and Bartini's (2001) finding that, at the end of middle school, girls nominated "dominant boys" as dates to a hypothetical party.

Popularity research supports these findings in that bullies and aggressive peers are not always viewed negatively by other students and certainly are not socially rejected as perceived many years ago among aggression researchers. Instead, in some cases, aggressive kids and bullies are nominated as popular by their peers in elementary school (Rodkin, Farmer, Pearl, & Van Acker, 2000) and associate with individuals rated similarly in popularity and aggression (Farmer, Estell, Bishop, O'Neil, & Cairns, 2003; Farmer et al., 2002). As kids transition to middle school, aggressive and "tough boys" have also been nominated as cool by other aggressive boys and by some girls (Rodkin, Farmer, Pearl, & Van Acker, 2006).

It is important to understand how peers can, at times, also be a great source of support for children and adolescents. Peers can model prosocial and caring attitudes and behaviors. For example, adolescents with low levels of prosocial behaviors in sixth grade, relative to their friends, demonstrated improved prosocial behaviors at the end of eighth grade (Wentzel & Caldwell, 1997). Peers can also be sources of support when students are being victimized (Demaray & Malecki, 2002). In one study, peer victimization was not associated with internalizing and externalizing behavior problems for those youth with sufficient social support (Hodges & Perry, 1999).

FAMILIAL FACTORS

Families are the major socialization agent for young children. Parents, siblings, and other caregivers provide children with examples of learning emotions, regulating emotions, negotiating conflict, problem-solving situations, and developing other life skills. Unfortunately, children are sometimes presented with less than ideal role models and learn pro-aggression attitudes, develop an inability to identify or regulate emotions, learn a restricted range of emotional reactions to distressing situations (e.g., anger), and often fail to gain the necessary problem-solving or coping skills to manage situations at school and in their community. Climates of families vary substantially; however, there are some general observations regarding families who have children who are bullies, victims, or bully-victims. As a group, bullies report that their parents are more authoritarian, condone "fighting back," and use physical punishment (Baldry & Farrington, 2000; Loeber & Dishion, 1984; Olweus, 1995b), and these families have been described as lacking in warmth and structure, low in family cohesion, and high in family conflict (Oliver, Oaks, & Hoover, 1994; Olweus, 1993a; Stevens, De Bourdeaudhuji, & Van Oost, 2002).

Positive and negative attachments to parents have been found to be important in the emergence of bullying perpetration and victimization. Specifically, children who had insecure, anxious-avoidant, or anxious-resistant attachment styles at 18 months of age were more likely than children with secure attachments to become involved in bullying perpetration at ages 4 and 5 (Troy & Sroufe, 1987). On the other hand, McFadyen-Ketchum, Bates, Dodge, and Pettit (1996) found that aggressive children who experienced affectionate mother–child relationships showed significant decreases in aggressive/disruptive behaviors.

In a recent study examining factors that predicted bullying across the transition from elementary school to middle school, Espelage, Holt, Poteat, and VanBoven (in press) found that teacher attachment in fifth grade was a strong predictor of lower levels of bullying for students during their sixth-grade year, even after controlling for their level of bullying during their fifth-grade year. Furthermore, teacher attachment was the strongest predictor of lower levels of bullying, whereas other factors (e.g., parental attachment, social acceptance, and psychological functioning) were nonsignificant predictors after controlling for previous levels of bullying behavior. This finding provides additional support for the importance of the social context and students' interactions with not only their peers but also their teachers in accounting for and predicting their engagement in bullying behavior over a transitional period that can be difficult for many students.

Parental social support is another factor related to bullying involvement; middle school students classified as bullies and bully-victims indicated receiving substantially less social support from parents than students in the uninvolved group (Demaray & Malecki, 2003). There have been mixed findings with respect to family structure and bullying, with some studies showing a heightened risk for youth in nonintact families (Flouri & Buchanan, 2003) and others finding no association (Espelage et al., 2000). Finally, witnessing domestic violence and experiencing child maltreatment are associated with bullying perpetration (Baldry, 2003; Shields & Cicchetti, 2001).

A unique set of family characteristics exists for victims of bullying. Families of victims often have high levels of cohesion (Bowers, Smith, & Binney, 1994). Further, victims are more likely to have less authoritative parents (Smith & Myron-Wilson, 1998) and live in families in which there are low levels of negotiation (Oliver et al., 1994) and high levels of conflict (Mohr, 2006). Some evidence suggests that family structure and income are associated with being victimized by peers. In particular, in a study of Nordic children, both living in a single-parent home and having a low socioeconomic status family were associated with increased odds of being bullied (Nordhagen, Nielsen, Stigum, & Kohler, 2005). Further, as summarized by Duncan (2004), there appear to be some family characteristics of victims that vary by the child's gender. For instance, whereas male victims often have overly close relationships with their mothers, female victims are more likely to have mothers who withdraw love. Finally, peer victimization is associated with greater victimization in other domains, such as child maltreatment (Holt, Finkelhor, & Kaufman Kantor, 2007).

Less research has focused on family environments of bully-victims, although evidence suggests that parents of bully-victims tend to be less warm and more overprotective than parents of uninvolved youth and provide inconsistent discipline and monitoring (Schwartz, Dodge, Pettit, & Bates, 1997; Smith, Bowers, Binney, & Cowie, 1993). In addition, families of bully-victims are characterized by low levels of cohesion, although not as low as cohesion levels in families of bullies (Bowers et al., 1994).

A growing body of literature has assessed the influence of sibling aggression. Duncan (1999) surveyed 375 middle school students, 336 of whom had siblings. According to the results, 42% reported that they often bullied their siblings, 24% reported they often pushed

or hit their brothers and sisters, and 11% stated that they often beat up their siblings. A smaller group (30%) reported that siblings frequently victimized them, with 22% stating they were often hit or pushed around and 8% reporting they were often beaten up by a sibling. What is most pertinent to this discussion is the finding that 57% of bullies and 77% of bully-victims reported also bullying their siblings. A previous study by Bowers et al. (1994) detected a similar pattern of relations, finding that youth who bullied others reported negative and ambivalent relationships with siblings and viewed their siblings as more powerful than themselves. The opposite was found for victimized youth, who reported enmeshed and positive relationships with their siblings (Bowers et al., 1994).

SCHOOL FACTORS

Social control theory is a dominant theory in the literature to explain the development of both prosocial and antisocial behavior (Hirschi, 1969). This theory postulates that as individuals establish connections with conventional institutions within society (e.g., schools, churches, community organizations), they are less prone to wrongdoing and more likely to internalize norms of appropriate conduct. A conventional institution that is experienced by most children at a young age is school. Positive school bonding has been associated with lowered risk of student substance abuse, truancy, and other acts of misconduct (Hawkins, Catalano, & Miller, 1992). However, considerable debate has emerged over many decades about what aspects of the school environment make a difference in buffering any negative family or community factors to which children are exposed. Early research focused on tangible, physical aspects of the school environment, including teacher–student ratio, population, and budget (Griffith, 1996; Huber, 1983; Rutter, Maughan, Mortimore, Ouston, & Smith, 1979), with inconsistent associations with these factors and academic outcomes for students.

More recent research has focused on expanding school influence investigations to include broader constructs such as school policies, teacher attitudes, and the general ethos of a school as potential predictors of children's academic, social, and psychological development. Kasen and colleagues have produced the vast majority of the research in the past 17 years on the relation among school climate factors (Kasen, Berenson, Cohen, & Johnson, 2004; Kasen, Cohen, & Brook, 1998; Kasen, Johnson, & Cohen, 1990). In their earliest work, Kasen et al. (1990) found that students (ages 6–16 years) who went to schools with high rates of student–student and teacher–student conflict had significantly greater increases in oppositional, attentional, and conduct problems, whereas those from "well-organized, harmonious schools" that emphasized learning reported decreases in these outcomes. A follow-up study involving this sample found that students from the highly conflictual schools were at increased risk for alcohol abuse and a criminal conviction 6 years later (Kasen et al., 1998).

School climate is emerging as an extremely important influence on bullying/victimization. Kasen et al.'s (2004) study is perhaps the most comprehensive examination of the impact of school climate on changes in verbal and physical aggression, anger, and school problem indices. In this study, 500 children (and their mothers) across 250 schools were surveyed at the ages of 13½ and 16 years across a 2½-year interval. A 45-item school climate survey included multiple scales assessing social and emotional features of the school environment, including a conflict scale (classroom control, teacher–student conflict), learning focus scale, social facilitation scale, and student authority scale (student has say in politics and planning) as predictors. Outcome measures included a wide range of scales, including school problems, deviance, rebelliousness, anger, physical and verbal aggression, and bullying. Results found that after controlling for baseline aggression, students in highly conflictual schools had an increase in verbal and physical aggression. In contrast, attendance at schools that emphasized learning resulted in a decrease in aggression and other school-related problems. Of particular interest was the finding that schools high in informal relations had increases in bullying perpetration over the 2½-year interval and schools with high conflict and high informality combined had the highest increase in bullying over time.

School climate is a particularly important variable to consider because adult supervision decreases from elementary to middle school. In turn, less structure and supervision are associated with concomitant increases in bullying rates among middle school students, in particular in locations such as playgrounds and lunchrooms (Craig & Pepler, 1997). Additionally, bullying occurs at a higher rate in hallways between classes (AAUW, 2001) and other places where students often report feeling unsafe and afraid (Astor, Meyer, & Pitner, 2001). Astor and colleagues (2001) offer additional insights into how students and teachers in both elementary and middle schools perceive public spaces in their schools as violence-prone locations. In that study, these authors drew on theories of territoriality and undefined public spaces to argue that bullying and other violent acts are more likely to occur in undefined public spaces (e.g., hallways, stairwells) than in places that are more defined as being someone's territory (e.g., classrooms). As part of the study, students in five elementary schools and two middle schools in grades 2, 4, 6, and 8 were presented with maps of their school and asked to identify places where they felt unsafe or they felt were dangerous.

Qualitative and quantitative analyses supported the early school climate work but also provided some new information that has direct prevention implications for school administrators. It was not surprising that students in all schools perceived places lacking in adult supervision and monitoring as unsafe. Crowding and bullying were consistently mentioned as reasons for feeling unsafe. Middle school students reported feeling less safe than elementary school students and were not certain which adults they could turn to for help. Similarly, middle school teachers reported greater conflict in their role in monitoring public spaces. Although middle school students reported feeling unsafe in most undefined public spaces, elementary school students reported feeling less safe on playgrounds than middle school students. These results suggest that bullying could be decreased in schools by first understanding where bullying is happening through Astor et al.'s (2001) mapping procedure. These data could then be used to develop an increase in monitoring of the high-frequency areas.

Bullying also occurs within the confines of the classroom. As such, it is clear that classroom practices and teachers' attitudes are also salient components of school climate that contribute to bullying prevalence. Aggression varies from classroom to classroom, and in some instances aggression is supported. For example, researchers have found levels of aggression in elementary school to significantly differ across classrooms (Henry et al., 2000; Kellam, Ling, Merisca, Brown, & Ialongo, 1998), and those aggressive students in classrooms with norms supportive of aggression become

more aggressive over time compared with students in less aggressive classrooms. Bullying tends to be less prevalent in classrooms where most children are included in activities (R. S. Newman, Murray, & Lussier, 2001), teachers display warmth and responsiveness to children (Olweus et al., 1999), and teachers respond quickly and effectively to bullying incidents (Olweus, 1993a, 1993b). Furthermore, Hoover and Hazler (1994) note that when school personnel tolerate, ignore, or dismiss bullying behaviors, they are conveying implicit messages about values that victimized students internalize. Additionally, students who bully others tend to do so when adults are not around.

SOCIETAL CONSEQUENCES

Certainly, being bullied or bullying others is not unique to American schools; it has been identified as a common occurrence in other venues, including workplaces and prisons. Even within the best practices of prevention, bullying is not likely to simply go away, and it is clear from some of the literature discussed in this chapter that there are major incentives for children and adolescents who bully others and often little support for the victims. The bottom line is that sometimes bullies are effective in using their aggression to get what they want, and this behavior is likely to continue into their intimate relationships and their working relationships. For example, there are some preliminary data that kids who bully their peers in late elementary school are more likely to be identified as students who sexually harass their peers in middle school (Pelligrini, 2002b) and are also more likely to report being verbally and physically abusive in dating relationships (Connolly, Pepler, Craig, & Taradash, 2000). Although a substantial amount of research needs to be conducted to substantiate a connection between these forms of aggression, preliminary evidence suggests that there might be something similar in the underlying phenomena. These studies and this research are expanded in the next chapter as we take on the discussion of bullying as a social relationship problem.

CONCLUSIONS AND RECOMMENDATIONS

In this chapter, factors that relate to the development and continuation of bullying perpetration and victimization have been introduced and discussed briefly. It is clear from the literature that bullying emerges as a result of a multitude of factors, including a child's personality, home environment, peers, and experiences at school. Children and adolescents who are at risk for engaging in bullying behaviors or are who at risk for being victimized report experiencing multiple risk factors and have fewer protective experiences. It is clear from the research that there are several "stopping points" for children to not become a bully, bully-victim, or victim. That is, social support, supportive friends, a positive school climate, involvement in extracurricular activities, and a supportive family all serve to protect or buffer children from both experiencing and expressing bullying, and these factors also serve to minimize the psychological impact of these deleterious behaviors (see Figure 2.1).

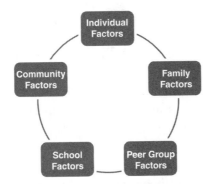

What are some interventions that you can do at each "stopping point"?

Social-Ecological Factors	Y/N?	Y/N?	Y/N?	Y/N?	Make a list
Individual Factors	Individual counseling?	Group counseling?	Working with school psychologists, counselors, and social workers?	Teach healthy problem solving and conflict resolution?	Other?
Family Factors	Work with parents/caregivers?	Encourage parental involvement?	Report any suspected neglect or abuse?	Create a supportive climate for parents?	Other?
Peer Group Factors	Teach about the negative consequences of bullying?	Actively intervene in the peer group and break apart negative groups?	Identify and reward positive leaders?	Create conditions in your school where bullying is not rewarded?	Other?
School Factors	Treat all adults and students with respect?	Adults intervene consistently when they see bullying?	Students who bully others are helped and taught how to change their behaviors?	The school climate is positive?	Other?
Community Factors	Community leaders work together to create a positive community?	Community resources are used to support schools and families?	Community–school partnerships are in place?	Schools are a vibrant part of the community?	Other?

FIGURE 2.1. Social-ecological model of bullying/victimization: Interventions.

CASE EXAMPLE: ANDREW

Andrew was identified for the gifted program at his school as a first grader. He had performed well in all academic areas until he reached middle school. After transitioning to middle school, his grades started falling. His love of learning and his enthusiasm for school diminished rapidly. In addition, Andrew began complaining of stomachaches and headaches on school days. His parents tried to talk with Andrew, but he always said everything was fine. His teachers provided little insight, and during fall conferences they even questioned whether there was something at home that was stressing him out.

Frustrated with the situation, Andrew's parents took him to his pediatrician for a physical. His pediatrician indicated that he was in excellent health and referred him for an eye exam. His vision checked out fine as well. After ruling out medical and vision difficulties, Andrew's doctor suggested that they schedule an appointment with a child psychologist to rule out possible psychological difficulties such as depression. Andrew's parents were initially uncomfortable with the idea of taking him to a psychologist because they did not know what to expect. Additionally, Andrew was very resistant to the idea, insisting that he was fine. After receiving his first semester report card with several Fs, Andrew's parents scheduled an appointment with the psychologist.

Although Andrew was initially resistant to going to a psychologist, his parents stuck with the therapy sessions. He gradually began to build trust with his psychologist and started sharing more of what had been bothering him at school. Most of the boys in his small class had been excluding him from participating in activities. This had been occurring both in and outside of school. For example, one of the boys would plan a party and not invite Andrew. When Andrew would ask about the activity, he was often told that they were sorry and must have forgotten to invite him. Andrew struggled with wanting to believe that these were simple oversights. However, as this pattern continued, he came to recognize that these were not simple mistakes. Additionally, in the school setting, he was often told he could not sit at certain tables during lunch time or participate in certain activities during recess. Andrew talked to his psychologist about feeling ashamed and lonely. Initially he wanted to talk with his teachers and parents about this, but he started to worry about their reaction. He had concerns that they would think he was a "loser" or a "reject." His parents had a lot a friends, and Andrew assumed that they may also be embarrassed by his situation.

Thoughts about Andrew's Case

More and more children seem to fit Andrew's description. Many children who are bullied are embarrassed by what is happening. They are often reluctant to talk about what is happening with their parents or teachers. Boys in particular tend to view being bullied as a sign of their own weakness and seem to feel more shame. Additionally, they are often taught not to "tattle" and to handle situations on their own. They may keep their worries and stresses to themselves, which often results in a negative impact on their daily functioning. It is hard to perform up to your potential when you are worried, stressed, and upset. Andrew talked about not being able to concentrate on his schoolwork because he was so focused on the fact that he was being bullied by his classmates.

How do parents respond in this type of situation? From a young age, children need to feel as though their parents are there to listen to them and accept them no matter what the situation. Opportunities to learn how to express and talk about feelings are essential. Modeling open expression of feelings and working to create an environment in which children feel accepted are critical, as is following up on children's concerns. When significant changes are noted in behaviors, moods, or physical functioning, it is often indicative of a larger problem. In Andrew's case, his parents' instincts told them that they should not just accept his assertions that everything was fine. They took the steps to follow up with several different doctors, even though their son was quite resistant initially.

Once Andrew began talking with his psychologist and opening up about his problems, things began to improve. He was able to learn more effective coping skills to deal with difficult situations. Additionally, he was able to develop strategies for initiating and maintaining positive peer relationships.

FOLLOW-UP QUESTIONS

1. A social-ecological conceptualization of bullying encourages us to think about individual, peer, family, school, and societal factors that all interact to contribute to bullying behaviors. What were the social-ecological factors that contributed to this case?

2. After the transition to middle school, Andrew's grades dropped and he experienced psychosomatic complaints. His parents noted this change in behavior and took him to talk with a psychologist. Think about students you know who have displayed a change in behavior. Does your school have a referral system for these kids?

3. We often hear that when students are experiencing bullying in school, they don't tell adults for fear of being seen as weak and rejected. How can adults encourage students to express their feelings openly? What systems are in place at your school or home that encourage the sharing of feelings?

4. William Pollack, author of *Real Boys* (1998), writes that many boys are depressed and lonely and that our society forces them to suppress their true emotions. What supports exist for boys to talk about their feelings about being bullied or about bullying others? How might societal pressures that reward strength, power, and dominance send conflicting messages to our young people about the importance of healthy relationships and respect for all?

3

Understanding Bullying
as a Social Relationship Problem

Why is it that children cannot just get along? Why is being respectful something that has to be taught at every turn of child development? Why do children choose to humiliate, embarrass, and terrorize one another rather than encouraging and supporting one another? These questions are addressed in detail in this chapter. Our premise is that bullying and peer victimization are social and societal problems. Moreover, bullying and peer victimization need to be seen as a collective social problem. Bullying and other forms of peer victimization are attitudes and behaviors that all humans should be concerned with, not just parents of school-age children. This premise means that bullying is a social problem that affects *everyone*. In this chapter, we outline the major incentives that are associated with being involved in bullying in our schools and communities. We discuss how involvement in bullying, as a bully, victim, or bully-victim, creates a society in which children and adolescents are unaffected by disrespect and disregard for others. Our children and adolescents are too often numb to disrespect, and this serves to only perpetuate bullying as social relationship problem (Pepler, Craig, & O'Connell, in press). This disrespect does not go away when our students are handed their high school diploma; these attitudes and behaviors are taken into dating relationships, work environments, familial contexts, and community settings. Therefore, it behooves us to conceptualize bullying and peer victimization as societal issues, not just school issues.

BULLYING, SOCIAL SKILLS DEFICIT, AND THEORY OF MIND

To comprehend how children's involvement in bullying is a social problem, we must start with a discussion of the internal cognitive and emotional aspects associated with bullying that lay the foundation for bullying as a social problem and interfere with the development of healthy and respectful friendships and relationships in the future. For many decades, both the basic and applied psychological literature left us with the impression that bullies

28

were socially unskilled and resorted to aggression only because they did not have the skills to initiate and maintain relationships. According to this model, the person who bullies others is generally an individual with low intelligence and a poor ability to negotiate social interactions, resorting to aggression because he or she knows no other way to solve social problems (Crick, 1999).

Viewed within a cognitive framework, deficits in social information processing were used to explain how children and adolescents became aggressive (Dodge, Pettit, McClaskey, & Brown, 1986). The social skills deficit model is based on research studies that found that aggressive individuals are more likely to manifest problems at any of the levels of social information processing. An encoding-related problem is known in the psychological literature as the "hostile attribution bias" (Coie & Dodge, 1998), and it is based on research findings that suggest aggressive individuals are more likely to interpret ambiguous social cues as malevolent. With respect to representation and processing, it is generally assumed that aggressive children have a poor understanding of others' mental states, have poor self-control, and are deficient in judgments, which then result in impulsive and potentially violent behavior (Berkowitz, 1993).

Although this description may correctly capture the characteristics of some bullies and/or bully-victims, it is questionable whether the social skills deficit model should be embraced as a generic model for all types of aggression, especially bullying. In other words, this social skills deficit model (Dodge & Coie, 1987) continues to dominate the psychological literature, but there is increasing awareness among bully prevention scholars and clinicians that this model does not fit all who are involved in bullying. Another alternative that could be useful in terms of understanding at least an important subset of the bullying behaviors is the one offered by the approach within the frame of theory of mind (Sutton, Smith, & Swettenham, 1999). It is documented that theory of mind begins to develop as early as age 3 or 4. Being able to understand that there can be two different realities (the real and the imagined) and to be able to manipulate them (e.g., pretense) is a necessary condition (a prestage) to developing a theory of mind.

Research has been conducted for years on the development of theory of mind in children (Astington, Harris, & Olson, 1988). Studies involve deception and storytelling methods and have compared children with average intelligence with developmentally delayed children and autistic children. These studies found that children older than 4 years performed significantly better than the children younger than 4 on deception and storytelling tasks, and children with no developmental delays outperformed autistic and mentally retarded children. It appears then that children with no developmental delays had a deeper understanding of the mental and emotional states of the characters involved in the story and these skills improved with age.

Now, let's turn back to how theory of mind relates to bullying. It is important to think about what bullying entails. Bullying is a repetitive act, based on an imbalance in power between a bully (or bullies) and a chosen victim, who plays the role of a constant target for aggression. This act is social in nature in that it usually takes place among a relatively permanent group of students. A theory of mind conceptualization of bullying recognizes that bullying is social in nature and involves the bully actively seeking out his or her victim (Sutton et al., 1999). Many studies indicate that most of the victims are usually children who are disliked by many of their peers. It is not politically correct to suggest that some children have physical and personality characteristics that place them at risk for victimization, but it is true. Children and adolescents who bully others do, in fact, pick their victims very carefully. This selection or choice might be the result of a judgment that makes use of a real understanding of the victim's weaknesses and of how this child is perceived by other classmates. In other words, making use of a correct attribution of mental states or having a heightened theory of mind makes the bully/victim pairing successful (Sutton et al., 1999).

Another aspect that suggests an understanding of mental states on the part of the bully is the fact that many times bullies work deliberately to build a reputation among their peers through being "tough" and controlling of other people (Salmivalli et al., 1996). When using indirect or relational forms of bullying, bullies use subtle methods to hurt the victim, such as rumors, opinion manipulation, irony, and teasing, all of which are conducive to the exclusion of the victim from the social group. It is clear that the "success" of this kind of bullying relies on a sound understanding of other peoples' beliefs and different perspectives. These individuals understand how attitudes and perceptions of others can be changed and manipulated through deception and hurtful behavior.

The most important implication of Sutton and colleagues' argument is that an explanatory theory of bullying not only has to attend to the cognitive ability of those involved but should also consider emotions and values (Sutton et al., 1999) of all participants. If bullies do have the ability to read their environment and manipulate others, it appears that we should figure out why it is that they would use these heightened skills to harm others. Sutton and colleagues argue that bullies do not value prosocial attitudes and behaviors. It appears that bullies, bully-victims, and others involved do not have empathy for their victims (Sutton et al., 1999). Take, for example, a study conducted by Borg (1998) focusing on the role of emotions in aggression. This study found that only 49.8% of the bullies reported feeling sorry for a victim of bullying, whereas 40.6% claimed to be indifferent and 20.9% reported feeling satisfaction after a bullying event. Interestingly, the secondary schoolchildren, ages 11 to 14 years, were more likely to report feeling indifferent and satisfied than younger children (Borg, 1998).

Another study examined perceptions related to feelings of individuals involved in bullying (Smith et al., 1993). These researchers presented students with videotaped episodes of bullying and asked them to describe the feelings of the bullies and the victims who were involved in the scenarios. Children (ages 9–11 years) were categorized into bully, victim, and uninvolved groups based on peer nominations. Among bullies, 80%, in contrast to only 30% of the uninvolved or victims, described the videotaped bullies as feeling happy, whereas only 27% of the bullies and 53% of the controls and victims described the victims as being unhappy (Smith et al., 1993).

In a more recent study, Menesini and colleagues (2003) investigated differences between bullies, victims, and uninvolved students with respect to their attributions of moral emotions and the reasoning that led to these attributions in fictional bullying situations. Participants (ages 9–13 years) were categorized into bully, victim, and outsider groups based on their responses to an adapted version of the Participant Roles Questionnaire (Salmivalli et al., 1996). The students were presented with a story of bullying using a set of 10 cartoons depicting typical bullying situations (e.g., consistent imbalance in power between the aggressor and the victim) and were asked, "If you were the bully, what would you feel and why?" Children's responses were clustered into six categories: egocentric responsibility (e.g., "I would feel guilty because the teachers could punish me later on"), conventional rules (e.g., "If I were the bully, I would feel guilty because I'm doing bad things"), empathy for the victim, egocentric disengagement (e.g., "I would not feel guilty because it was a joke"), deviant rules (e.g., "The others do the same"), and absence of empathy for the victim. Students who bullied others reported more emotions of disengagement than victims and uninvolved students, and these students were more likely than victims and uninvolved students to mention egocentric responsibility accompanied with guilt and shame and egocentric disengagement as a justification for moral disengagement. Even the 30% of bullies who were aware of the negative effects on the victims were more concerned about personal consequences such as punishment (Menesini et al., 2003).

These findings indicate that some students who bully others are emotionally self-centered, fail to feel for their victims, and lack feelings of remorse. This speaks to the necessity of considering the emotional aspects in addition to the cognitive components of bullying. These findings, taken together, suggest that bullies do not necessarily lack social skills but might have advanced cognitive skills. They appear to understand the difference between right and wrong; they just simply do not care about being respectful to others. When faced with the thought of being punished, they might also resort to deception and self-protection. So how do we as a society begin to shift this attitude and apathy that is emerging in our children and adolescents?

EMPATHY, CARING, AND A WILLINGNESS TO INTERVENE

One could take from this literature the importance of teaching those who bully others to care or empathize with their victims. Certainly, for some bullies, this might be an appropriate strategy. This is not a new idea. Thus, we turn to the research on the relation between bullying and empathy. Research has consistently found negative associations between empathy and aggression, and a positive correlation between empathy and prosocial skills (Feshbach & Feshbach, 1982; Kaukiainen et al., 1999; Mehrabian, 1997; Miller & Eisenberg, 1988). Empathy includes one's emotional reaction to another individual's state that consists of experiencing the perceived emotional state vicariously (Mehrabian & Epstein,

1972). The general consensus among scholars is that empathic responses rely on both cognitive and emotional processes. The cognitive component relates to taking the perspective of others (Davis, 1983), whereas the emotional dimension refers to affective reactions to the emotional states of others (Feshbach & Feshbach, 1982).

The association among aggression, prosocial behavior, and empathy supports the importance of discriminating between the cognitive and emotional factors. For example, the inverse correlation between aggression and empathy was found to be stronger in studies that focused on the emotional component of empathy than studies in which cognitive empathy was measured (Endresen & Olweus, 2001; Mehrabian, 1997). Davis (1983) found that empathic concern (e.g., affective reaction to the other's emotional state with a focus on the other), but not perspective taking, was related to helping behavior (Davis, 1983). Similarly, Hoffman (2000) argued that a child who has high abilities in perspective taking but no willingness or ability to share the perceived feelings of others is more likely to become unscrupulously cunning. Prevention efforts need to more accurately recognize the variability in empathy skills that children and adolescents have.

The relation between empathy and aggression, including bullying, is further complicated by sex differences. In general, research has found that females score higher on empathy measures than males (Cohen & Strayer, 1996; Endresen & Olweus, 2001), especially on scales related to emotional measures of empathy (Cohen & Strayer, 1996). Additionally, the relation between aggression and empathy occurs differently in females than in males (Cohen & Strayer, 1996; Espelage, Mebane, & Adams, 2004). For example, Espelage and colleagues found that, for females, empathic concern was more strongly negatively correlated with relational aggression than with bullying. In contrast, for males, empathic concern was more strongly negatively correlated with bullying than with relational aggression. Another interesting observation was that perspective taking significantly predicted bullying only for girls (Espelage et al., 2004). Therefore, these findings suggest that decreasing bullying among both girls and boys will involve prevention efforts that are sensitive to gender differences in empathy.

In some ways, this goes back to the issue of values or attitudes toward bullying. Endresen and Olweus (2001) conducted a study that explored specifically the association between empathy and bullying, but they introduced an important third variable: attitudes toward bullying. Using a sample of 2,286 students in grades 6 to 9 (ages 13–16 years), the investigators found that empathic concern was negatively and modestly correlated with bullying, but it was more strongly associated with positive attitudes toward bullying. The investigators suggested that attitudes toward bullying might mediate the relation between empathy and bullying. In a more recent study, Espelage and colleagues (2004) found that a positive attitude toward bullying partially mediated the relation between empathic concern and bullying for males and the relation between perspective taking and bullying for both males and females.

These findings support Sutton's speculation that not only do cognitive factors play an important role in bullying, but other factors, including empathy, values, and attitudes, are also important. The role of affect and emotional development is important in understanding bullying, especially in the context in which the aggressor has a heightened theory of mind. A legitimate question in this situation is what exactly makes the difference between merely understanding the victim's mind and emotion and feeling for that person, so that the bully would choose to stop the hurtful behavior? In the research literature, a distinction has been made between empathy, as feeling *with* others, and sympathy, as feeling *for* others.

Another aspect of affect that must be taken into consideration is related to the values that bullies hold, how they view aggression, and what kind of possible reinforcement they receive. Past research has shown that aggressive individuals tend to hold the belief that aggression is a socially acceptable behavior and that the display of aggressive behavior supports the positive beliefs about it, thereby increasing the likelihood of repeating the behavior (Anderson & Bushman, 2002). Combine this with the socializing aspects of bullying and the fact that aggressive children/adolescents are seen as attractive by their same and opposite sex (as described in more detail in Chapter 2), and it is not a mystery that there are many "kudos" for being labeled as a bully.

Indeed, in a recent edited book entitled *Aggression and Adaptation: The Bright Side to Bad Behavior* (Hawley, Little, & Rodkin, 2007), aggression researchers take on the question, "When is aggression adaptive?" Psychological, sociological, and biological literature has consistently documented that aggression can be and is adaptive. Historians would not ponder the importance of violence and aggression in the development of countries, governments, and industries. However, for some reason, parents, teachers, and psychologists have had to argue that aggression is not adaptive. Smith (2007) argues beautifully for a different way of thinking about aggression and bullying as adaptive versus maladaptive. He outlines many theories that support the idea that bullying and relational aggression are related to increased dominance in peer groups, increased popularity among peers, and increased popularity of dating among middle school students. However, he then goes on to draw an important distinction. Aggression and bullying have been labeled as socially deviant by scholars and clinicians from many disciplines, but they are not developmentally deviant.

Adding to this discussion, Rodkin and Wilson (2007) argue that the aggression-as-adaptive framework has been virtually ignored by developmental psychologists. In contrast, the focus has been on identifying maladaptive aspects of aggression and bullying, including poor social cognition, deficits in selective information processing, and so on. Rodkin and Wilson suggest that focusing on the maladaptive aspects of aggression might be more palatable to consumers of potential prevention programs, including parents, teachers, and school administrators. Perhaps the reason that many of our bullying prevention programs are not effective is partly due to ignoring that this form of aggression is adaptive and plays an important role in improving the social status of children. Thus, it is our point in this chapter that bullying has not been accurately conceptualized. If we continue to incorrectly focus on bullying as maladaptive, then we are losing the opportunity to understand how prevention efforts can work within the social nature of bullying in order to truly stop these behaviors.

Because of the focus on aggression as maladaptive, it is not surprising that bullying perpetration has not been eradicated in our schools, homes, communities, and workplaces. It could be related to the important role that bystanders play in sustaining bullying in schools and the lack of students' willingness to intervene. In a recent study, Espelage and colleagues examined the associations among sex, empathy, attitudes toward bullying, willingness to intervene, and bullying within peer groups in a sample of 565 sixth- to eighth-grade students (Espelage & Green, in press). Correlational analyses demonstrated that empathic con-

cern and perspective taking were associated with less self-reported bullying and fighting, and a positive attitude toward bullying was associated with less willingness to intervene. Regression analyses indicated that empathy (empathic concern and perspective taking) mediated the association between a positive attitude toward bullying and willingness to intervene.

Peer groups were identified via social network analysis, and hierarchical linear modeling supported correlational analysis in that empathy and attitudes toward bullying were highly associated with willingness to intervene within peer groups. Additionally, this willingness to intervene was further explained by peer group-level bullying in male peer groups, but there was no peer effect to model for female peer groups. Thus, prevention programs need to address the lack of willingness to intervene that is reinforced by adolescent peer groups.

Even more disturbing is the failure to reduce bullying in the schools and its correlate with other forms of problematic behaviors through adolescence and adulthood, including conduct problems, sexual harassment, dating violence, alcohol/drug use, and so on. It is not hard to imagine that if children and adolescents lack basic empathy for others, they might become involved in other forms of deviant behavior. In fact, research suggests that students who bully others are more likely than their peers to engage in externalizing behaviors, to experience conduct problems, and to be delinquent (Haynie et al., 2001; Nansel et al., 2001). In addition, if we envision bullying as a societal problem and a social problem, then we have to recognize that children leave these experiences lacking the skills necessary to manage subsequent life experiences, namely how to negotiate interpersonal relationships. Additionally, bullying is strongly associated with both alcohol and drug use. In their study of fifth to eighth graders, Pepler, Craig, Connolly, and Henderson (2002) found that, for both boys and girls, bullies were almost five times more likely to report alcohol use and seven times more likely to report drug use than nonbullies.

BULLYING AND THE CONNECTION TO SEXUAL HARASSMENT

Research is also beginning to establish a link between peer violence and sexual violence perpetration. Although the question of whether bullies go on to sexually harass their peers or engage in sexual assault needs to be better studied, there are some common correlates with bullying (as described in Chapter 2). Adolescents who engage in sexual assault have positive attitudes toward violence, come from homes where violence is modeled, have a need for dominance or control in relationships, and have generally low levels of empathy. Certainly, a conversation about the overlap of predictors of these behaviors is beyond the current state of the literature, yet we do have some evidence that bullying and sexual violence perpetration are related. Our literature search revealed three empirical studies that demonstrate an association between peer aggression and various types of sexual violence.

Ozer, Tschann, Pasch, and Flores (2004) longitudinally studied 16- to 20-year-old Mexican American and European American males and females. They focused on peer violence (e.g., fighting with another teenager) and sexual aggression (including unwanted touching and unwanted intercourse) and found that, for males, engaging in peer violence was associated with sexual aggression perpetration at Time 1 and 1 year later and perpetrating sexual violence at Time 1 was modestly associated with peer violence perpetration at Time 2. Although their study did not show a significant association between peer aggression at Time 1 and later sexual aggression at Time 2, it did provide evidence that both peer violence and sexual violence perpetration are associated. Other studies have also shown that bullying and sexual harassment are related (DeSouza & Ribeiro, 2005; Pepler et al., 2006).

DeSouza and Ribeiro (2005) examined a sample of Brazilian high school students and found that, for both males and females, bullying peers was associated with sexually harassing the same peers. Pepler and colleagues (2006) found a positive association between bullying and sexual harassment perpetration among students. In this cross-sectional study of 961 elementary school (grades 6–8) and 935 middle school students (grades 9–12), sexual harassment perpetration was more prevalent among students who bullied others than those who did not report bullying others. Examining the relationship between bullying and sexual harassment longitudinally, Pellegrini (2001) found that boys who bullied peers at the beginning of grade 6 were also likely to sexually harass peers at the end of grade 7 ($r = .44$, $p < .0001$), but this association was mediated by self-reported high dating frequency at the end of grade 6. To our knowledge, no studies to date have examined the links between bullying and other forms of sexual violence beyond sexual harassment (i.e., unwanted touching, rape, or attempted rape).

CONCLUSIONS AND RECOMMENDATIONS

In this chapter, research has been presented that encourages readers to think about bullying as a special case of aggression that is largely a social problem (see Figure 3.1). Bullying is an interactional style that benefits the perpetrators and serves to socialize those surrounding the bullies, who might be leaders in the peer group. Recent research has found that bullies can be socially skilled, have normal to heightened theory of mind, are in some cases viewed as popular in friendship groups, and are sought after as students begin dating relationships. Many prevention programs have focused on empathy training to prevent bullying, but this practice fails to consider research findings showing that not all bullies lack empathy but, instead, they do not value prosocial behavior. Prevention programs, therefore, need to focus

You hear a student say . . .	What you could say . . .

You're not invited to my birthday party!

That's not a very nice thing to say. Let's work this out.

Hey, let's all get together tonight and not invite Sarah!

I couldn't help but overhear that you're not inviting Sarah—how do you think she might feel?

I'm going to beat up Matthew after school today. Come and watch!

Do you realize that if you harm Matthew legal charges will be brought against you?

Fill in your own examples . . .

FIGURE 3.1. Suggestions for modeling healthy communication.

on changing the positive attitudes toward bullying along with the empathy and perspective-taking training. Barriers to students' willingness to intervene also need to be identified to maximize the effectiveness of bullying prevention programs. Bullying perpetration does not go away when students go onto high school, and it does not go away when students receive their high school diploma. Research suggests that bullying perpetration is related to other forms of violence and misconduct; thus, bullying should be viewed as a special case of violence that places students at risk for other forms of aggression and violence as adults.

CASE EXAMPLE: GEORGE

George was a voracious reader. He could read books at the high school level even though he was only in third grade. He also had an excellent memory. He could tell you everything you ever wanted to know about "Star Wars." He knew every character and had memorized almost all of the lines from the movies. Yet he could not seem to develop appropriate peer relationships. He struggled with reading social cues, and many of his classmates found him to be annoying. Since beginning school, he had gradually become the focus of much teasing and bullying from his peers. To make matters worse, he did not have an athletic bone in his body. He was uncoordinated and awkward.

This combination of factors led to George being the target of much bullying and aggression from his classmates in his small school. The daily routine at recess involved a game of "Smear the Queer," and George was always the one to get "smeared." They would throw dirt at his pants and yell "Smear the queer." His parents knew George struggled socially but did not realize the extent of his difficulties until he began having night terrors. Soon after, he also began throwing up in the mornings before school. He had told his parents that he hated school, but they had not realized the extent of his difficulties.

George's parents were sure things would work out, and they went to talk with the school teacher and principal. They were met with a lot of resistance and felt as though the school was blaming their son's behavior for the bullying. The principal suggested that George should work on his athletic skills so he could keep up with the other boys at recess. Additionally, the school defended the playing of games such as "Smear the Queer," stating that these were typical activities for boys this age. They also suggested that George could stay in from recess if he felt more comfortable. George's parents were frustrated, and repeated attempts to work with the school were ineffective.

After much deliberation, George's parents decided to take him out of the school. There were no other school options in their small town, so they planned on home schooling George until they could come up with another plan. When they approached the school about this idea, they were shocked when it was suggested that they could be reported for child neglect if they refused to send him to school.

After a few weeks of home schooling, George's night terrors stopped and he began feeling better. They started seeing their old George again. However, they still felt angry and betrayed by the school system that was supposed to help them, that their taxes paid for, and that they trusted. Additionally, they knew that George needed some more socialization opportunities and that home schooling was not a long-term solution for their son.

Thoughts about George's Case

George's parents are not unique in their situation. Many times the very school system that parents feel should be there for their children does not openly accept the fact that bullying is occurring. Many parents and children feel as though they are blamed when the children are bullied.

FOLLOW-UP QUESTIONS

1. We argue that bullying is a relationship problem. In George's case, he was seen as "different" and didn't fit in with the other students. How does your school support students who are different? How do you as a teacher and/or parent teach respect for difference and tolerance for all people?

2. Socially, on the playground, the students at this school were not playing well with George. How does your school monitor playground behavior? What do you do to help teach students how to develop and maintain socially healthy relationships?

3. The school condoned the game "Smear the Queer," stating that it was just typical kids' play. When adults in schools, homes, and communities support negative and hurtful actions, children are left with a sense of confusion about appropriate behavior. How do you model appropriate behavior for your students?

4. Additionally, the game title, "Smear the Queer," is a derogatory, homophobic title. What is the impact of overtly or covertly accepting names that are derogatory and homophobic? Can you think of examples where you either corrected a student for saying "queer" or "gay," or are these terms commonplace in your school and community? What do you do to stand up to negative, degrading, and humiliating words?

5. Both George and his parents didn't feel that the school was supportive of their situation. Think of examples in your school where there is a conflict between the family and the school. The old adage "It takes two to tango" is quite true. What can the school personnel do to help reduce the adversarial relationship between the school and the family?

4

Developing and Implementing an Effective Anti-Bullying Policy

Susan M. Swearer, Susan P. Limber, *and* Rebecca Alley

As of July 2008, anti-bullying laws have been implemented in 33 states (Chapter 5).[1] Given the ongoing publicity regarding bullying among school-age youth, it is likely that this legislative trend will continue until all 50 states have adopted anti-bullying laws. However, regardless of a specific state mandating anti-bullying legislation or not, it is our belief that all schools should develop, implement, and follow anti-bullying policies. It is particularly important to create local policies that will address the unique structures and environments that are idiosyncratic to every school and community.

THE BENEFITS OF ANTI-BULLYING POLICIES

Well-written anti-bullying policies can lay the foundation for clear communication about expectations for appropriate behavior and consequences for bullying behaviors. Policies inform decision making regarding the consequences for bullying and allow school personnel, parents, and students to communicate uniformly about expectations and consequences. Taking the time to write and implement anti-bullying policies also communicates to the community the serious nature of bullying. Historically, in this country, antidiscrimination, harassment, and gun laws have laid the foundation for communicating that these are serious societal concerns. The same trend appears to be happening for bullying.

---

[1]Given that laws are rapidly changing, readers are encouraged to check states' websites for the most up-to-date information.

Susan P. Limber, PhD, MLS, is Associate Professor in the Institute on Family and Neighborhood Life at Clemson University, Clemson, South Carolina.

Rebecca L. Alley, JD, is the IRB Coordinator of the Office of Research Compliance at Clemson University, Clemson, South Carolina.

Not only should anti-bullying policies include language for student protection, but these policies should also be consistent with district policies that protect the adults in schools. The importance of having both workplace bullying and school bullying policies will serve to further communicate the serious nature of bullying. For example, the Ohio Department of Education's (2007) "Anti-Harassment, Anti-Intimidation, or Anti-Bullying Model Policy states, "The policy is based on the belief that Ohio schools must provide physically safe and emotionally secure environments for all students and all school personnel" (p. 3). Thus, this model policy includes provisions for both students and adults in the school community.

Despite the obvious benefit of anti-bullying policies, many schools, districts, and states do not have these policies. At a recent workshop on bullying, participants were asked to complete a brief survey asking the question "Does your school have an anti-bullying policy?" Of the 44 participants, 11 replied, "Yes," 12 said, "No," and 21 replied, "Not sure." Of the 12 "yes" responses, some of the comments about their school's policy included "Vaguely written, intertwined with harassment policy," "It's not used/enforced," "No tolerance," "Just don't do it," "Zero tolerance, but don't know specifics," and "First offense = stop it! Second offense = stop it, &$#*@$!" Thus, the general experience from these participants was that their schools did not have anti-bullying policies, and if they did, they were vague and individuals were unclear about the specifics of the policy.

Several of the participants mentioned that their schools adopted zero-tolerance policies for bullying. There is clear evidence that zero-tolerance policies are not effective for reducing bullying behaviors (APA Task Force on Zero Tolerance, 2007; Casella, 2003). In-school suspension, out-of-school suspension, and expulsion are not strategies that teach students not to bully others. In fact, zero-tolerance policies communicate to these students that they are rejected from the very institution that is supposed to teach them! Zero tolerance is a failed initiative (Skiba & Knesting, 2002). It does not help fix social relationship problems; thus, the bullying continues and may even increase in severity.

Given the lack of evidence that zero-tolerance policies are effective for

reducing bullying behaviors, we advocate the development of anti-bullying policies like the Ohio Department of Education's policy, which includes intervention strategies to help teach students how to change their behavior. If we view bullying as a social relationship problem (Chapter 3), then we must adopt strategies that focus on teaching students how to develop healthy social relationships.

Will policies help reduce bullying behaviors? During a recent discussion, one school administrator declared "Policies don't change behaviors. State mandates just give schools more work to do." Although there is a prevailing belief that policies may create additional work, it is our (and others') belief that policies promote change (Soutter & McKenzie, 2000). We have too often consulted with schools that have no anti-bullying policies and, therefore, no mechanism for mandating protection of those being bullied and for fostering change. In this chapter, we discuss policy development and implementation. It is our firm conviction that all schools should develop and implement anti-bullying policies.

POLICY DEVELOPMENT

We use the state of Nebraska anti-bullying bill (Nebraska Unicameral, 2008) process as an example. For the past 3 years, several Nebraska state legislators have proposed an anti-bullying bill, and each year the bill has not been approved. However, in 2008, the Nebraska legislature passed the anti-bullying bill, which mandates that, by July 1, 2009, each school district in Nebraska must develop and implement an anti-bullying policy, and the policy must be reviewed annually. However, if we consider the above quote by a school administrator as even partially representative of prevailing beliefs, how will this mandate fare across school districts in Nebraska? How can every school and community ensure that their school district develop and implement an effective anti-bullying policy? Parents, local school boards, and school administrators should be supportive and lead the efforts in developing and implementing anti-bullying policies. In this chapter, we outline several steps for effective policy development and implementation.

Step 1: Define Bullying Behaviors

A clear and appropriate definition of bullying is a critical component of any local bullying policy. As a general rule, in developing a bullying policy, school administrators should use the definition of bullying provided in their own state's statute. This will avoid confusion and possible inconsistency with state law. In those cases in which statutory definitions are perceived to be unclear or too narrow, school administrators may want to seek legal guidance to clarify or expand the definition of bullying used in their policy. For example, New Jersey legislators included the condition that harassment, intimidation, or bullying be "motivated either by an actual or perceived characteristic, such as race, color, religion, ancestry, national origin, gender, sexual orientation, gender identity and expression, or a mental, physical or sensory handicap, or by any other distinguishing characteristic" (*New Jersey Statutes Annotated*, 2006).

Perhaps recognizing the limitations of this definition, in its model policy, the State of New Jersey, Department of Education (2007) noted that school districts may choose to consider acts of bullying that are not motivated by the factors identified in the statute: "Some acts of bullying are simply one child exercising power and control over another" (p. 4). They go on to caution that "if the district chooses to consider acts of bullying not motivated by the factors identified in the authorizing statute, they should take care to ensure that any expansion of [these] factors should be consistent with the case law, Federal and State statutes, regulations and policies and the districts' board-approved policies and procedures" (p. 4).

Where no relevant state law exists or where a statute fails to define bullying, local school officials are encouraged to include a definition of bullying in their policy that is consistent with that used by researchers and practitioners (see the discussion in Chapter 5 on "Definitions") and that includes indirect as well as overt forms of bullying (Limber & Small, 2003). For example, the California Department of Education's sample policy (n.d.) notes that bullying may include "direct physical contact, such as hitting or shoving; verbal assaults, such as teasing or name-calling; and social isolation or manipulation."

Bullying should not be equated with harassment, and language should be avoided that implies that bullying must be motivated by perceived or actual characteristics of a victim (such as gender, race, color, national origin, or disability; Limber & Small, 2003). Drafters of local policies may want to clarify that the policy is not meant to prohibit student expression protected under the First Amendment. The Washington State School Safety Center (2002) sample policy notes that the policy "is not intended to prohibit expression of religions, philosophical, or political views, provided that the expression does not substantially disrupt the educational environment." The Maine School Management Association's sample policy (n.d.) clarifies that

> for the purpose of this policy, bullying does not mean mere teasing, put-downs, "talking trash," trading of insults, or similar interactions among friends, nor does it include expression of ideas or beliefs so long as such expression is not lewd, profane, or does not interfere with students' opportunity to learn, the instructional program, or the operations of the schools. (p. 2)

Step 2: Refer to Available Model Policies

To further guide schools and districts in establishing anti-bullying policies, 11 state statutes require the state department of education to create a model anti-bullying policy. As discussed in the next section, however, this requirement does not necessarily guarantee that the state department of education will provide these materials or that such materials will prove helpful to local school administrators attempting to conform with the law.

Model Policies

Although only 11 states currently require their state departments of education to create model anti-bullying policies, a number of other states (or state organizations) have made available model or sample policies to guide local administrators. Through website searches as well as conversations with employees of state departments of education, 16 such policies were located (see Table 4.1 for a listing and web links). Approximately half are referred to as "model" policies and half as "sample" policies. It is unclear whether there is a meaningful difference between these terms. Use of the term *model policy*, however, may somewhat more strongly convey that local educators are encouraged to embrace the recommended language.

Model/sample policies range from very brief statements about bullying that are part of larger model policies (e.g., Michigan) to in-depth treatments of the topic. The State of New Jersey, Department of Education (2007), for example, provides detailed information on 11 statutory requirements, suggests model language (where appropriate) for each, and then, for

TABLE 4.1. Anti-Bullying Legislation and Policies and Internet Resources

State	Statutes	Dept. of Ed. model/sample policy	Bd. of Ed. policy	Internet source for model/sample policies
Alabama				
Alaska	✓	✓		www.eed.state.ak.us/tls/SchoolSafety/bullying.htm
Arizona	✓			
Arkansas	✓	✓		arkedu.state.ar.us/commemos/static/fy0203/attachments/ Policy_Writing_Recs.doc
California	✓	✓		www.cde.ca.gov/ls/ss/se/samplepolicy.asp
Colorado	✓	✓		www.colorado.edu/cspv/safeschools/bullying/bullying_ casbpolicy.html
Connecticut	✓			
Delaware	✓			
District of Columbia				
Florida				
Georgia	✓			
Hawaii				
Idaho	✓	✓		www.sde.idaho.gov/site/safe_drugfree/docs/ HarrassmentFall2001.pdf
Illinois	✓			
Indiana	✓			
Iowa	✓	✓		www.iowa.gov/educate/content/view/942/1106
Kansas	✓			
Kentucky				
Louisiana	✓			
Maine	✓	✓		www.maine.gov/education/bullyingprevention/management. rtf
Maryland	✓			
Massachusetts				www.mass.gov/Cago/docs/Community/SSI/Children_ PolicyMASchoolDistricts.rtf
Michigan		✓	✓	www.michigan.gov/documents/ModelCode_75513_7.pdf
Minnesota	✓			
Mississippi				
Missouri	✓			
Montana			✓	
Nebraska			✓	
Nevada	✓			
New Hampshire	✓			
New Jersey	✓	✓		www.state.nj.us/njded/parents/bully.htm
New Mexico				
New York	✓			
North Carolina			✓	

(continued)

TABLE 4.1. *(continued)*

State	Statutes	Dept. of Ed. model/sample policy	Bd. of Ed. policy	Internet source for model/sample policies
North Dakota				
Ohio	✓	✓	✓	*www.ode.state.oh.us/GD/Templates/Pages/ODE/ODEDetail. aspx?Page=3&TopicRelationID=1287&Content=44259*
Oklahoma	✓			
Oregon	✓			
Pennsylvania				
Rhode Island	✓	✓		*www.ride.ri.gov/psi/docs/child_family/substance/ bullying%20guidance%20and%20modelpolicy%2011-21- 03.pdf*
South Carolina	✓			*ed.sc.gov/agency/offices/ssys/safe_schools/sdfsc/documents/ ModelBullyingPolicy_.doc*
South Dakota				
Tennessee	✓			
Texas	✓			
Utah				
Vermont	✓	✓		*www.state.vt.us/educ/new/pdfdoc/pgm_safeschools/pubs/ bullying_prevention_04.pdf*
Virginia	✓	✓		*www.doe.virginia.gov/VDOE/Instruction/Sped/stu_conduct. pdf*
Washington	✓	✓		*www.k12.wa.us/SafetyCenter/pubdocs/Prohibitionof HarassmentIntimidationandBullyingSampleProcedure 3207P.doc*
West Virginia	✓	✓	✓	*twvde.state.wv.us/policies/p4373.html*
Wisconsin				
Wyoming				

Note. These websites were last verified July 19, 2008. Because state departments of education and other groups frequently update their websites, the exact addresses for these Internet resources may change over time.

each requirement, notes "issues for a district to consider in developing a policy that fits its own unique situations and that is consistent with existing policies" (p. 2).

We next summarize and comment on elements of model/sample policies. In keeping with the approach of the State of New Jersey, Department of Education (2007), we encourage administrators to develop policies that are consistent with state law and, where possible, model/sample policies but that also take into account current knowledge about "best practices" in addressing and preventing bullying and their own local issues and concerns. For this reason, we do not recommend that administrators adopt any sample/model policy verbatim. Rather, we encourage the development of local policies through a dialogue that takes into careful consideration the input of all relevant stakeholders, including administrators, teachers, nonteaching staff, parents, and students. Language from existing sample/ model policies may serve as a useful starting point for these discussions.

STATEMENTS OF DISTRICT OBLIGATIONS TO STUDENTS/PROHIBITIONS AGAINST BULLYING

Most model/sample policies include opening statements that highlight the obligation of the school district to provide safe learning environments for students. These statements typically are followed by clear prohibitions against bullying and/or statements of purpose to address bullying. For example, in its recommendations for writing anti-bullying policies, the Arkansas Department of Education (n.d.) notes:

> The School District has an obligation to and is committed to providing a safe learning environment for each of its students. Student achievement is best attained in an atmosphere that is free from the fear of emotional and physical intimidations and threats. . . . This school will not tolerate any behavior that is classified under the definition of bullying and will take steps needed to eliminate such behavior.

Iowa's policy states:

> The board is committed to providing all students with a safe and civil school environment in which all members of the school community are treated with dignity and respect. To that end, the board has in place policies, procedures, and practices that are designed to reduce and eliminate bullying and harassment as well as processes and procedures to deal with incidents of bullying and harassment. (Iowa Department of Education, 2007, p. 1)

Many model/sample policies provide an explanation of where the policy applies (see, e.g., California, Colorado, Iowa, Maine, Ohio, Rhode Island, Vermont). The language in California's sample policy is illustrative:

> This policy applies to students on school grounds, while traveling to and from school or a school-sponsored activity, during the lunch period, whether on or off campus, and during a school-sponsored activity. (California Department of Education, n.d., p. 1)

Several states' sample policies (e.g., Iowa, Maine) also note that the policy may apply away from school grounds or school-sponsored events if the behavior substantially disrupts the academic programs, the management of the school, or the welfare of students. Rhode Island's policy is notable in its prohibitions against bullying that extend beyond the students who initiate the bullying. State educational officials acknowledged that "students who see an act of bullying, and who the encourage it, are themselves engaging in bullying" (Rhode Island Department of Education, n.d., p. 1). Recognizing the role that bystanders can play in supporting bullying behavior (see Hanish, Kochenderfer-Ladd, Fabes, Martin, & Denning, 2004; Olweus et al., 1999; Pelligrini, 2002a; Salmiavelli et al., 1996), we encourage administrators to include similar language in their own policies.

We also encourage the inclusion of language that prohibits bullying by adults within the school community. Iowa's sample policy (Iowa Department of Education, 2007), for example, expressly prohibits bullying and harassment of students "by students, school employees, and volunteers who have direct contact with students" (p. 1). Massachusetts' sample policy perhaps goes the farthest in noting that "it applies to all students, school committee members, school employees, independent contractors, school volunteers, parents and legal guardians of students, and visitors to District schools where the conduct occurs on school premises or in school-related activities" (Mass. Gov., n.d., pp. 1–2). Such language can send a strong message to students and adults alike that the school district takes *all* bullying behavior seriously.

As part of their prohibitions against bullying, several model/sample policies effectively highlight the harms that bullying may cause. Arkansas' model policy notes that "bullying is a destructive behavior that will erode the foundational principles on which a school is built." The Maine School Management Association's sample policy on bullying (n.d.) is perhaps the most specific in detailing possible harmful effects of bullying:

> Bullying is detrimental to student learning and achievement. It interferes with the mission of the schools to educate their students and disrupts the operations of the school. Bullying affects not only students who are targets but also those who participate and witness such behavior. (p. 1)

Step 3: Clearly Outline Reporting of Incidents

Reporting known or suspected bullying is an important component of any effort to address bullying, and clear reporting procedures should be outlined in any local bullying policies. Recognizing that 18 states currently require or recommend procedures for reporting of bullying incidents by staff (and, in some cases, students), we encourage local policymakers to carefully review their state laws to ensure that their procedures are consistent with state law. Most state model/sample policies also provide guidance regarding reporting of bullying by students and school staff. New Jersey's model language is illustrative:

> All school employees are required to report alleged violations of this policy to the principal or the principal's designee. All other members of the school community, including students, parents, volunteers and visitors, are encouraged to report any act that may be a violation of this policy. (State of New Jersey, Department of Education, 2007, p. 10)

It is important that reporting be encouraged for suspected bullying (or "alleged violations") and not only for bullying that has been directly witnessed. In developing reporting language, New Jersey administrators encourage local policymakers to consider that

> the goal of a reporting procedure is to encourage reports of alleged violations . . . by making the reporting process simple and non-threatening. The district should consider every mechanism available to them to facilitate reporting, including web-based reporting mechanisms and locked boxes located in areas of the school where reports can be submitted without fear of being observed. (State of New Jersey, Department of Education, 2007, p. 10)

Several states' model policies take such concerns into consideration by providing systems for both in-person and anonymous reporting by students (e.g., New Jersey, Ohio, Vermont). A number of model policies also expressly prohibit retaliation against individuals who report suspected bullying (e.g., Arkansas, California, Iowa, Maine, New Jersey, Rhode Island, South Carolina) and/or note that individuals who knowingly fabricate reports may be subject to disciplinary action (e.g., Arkansas, Maine, New Jersey, Rhode Island, South Carolina, Washington).

Although an important component of bullying policies, reporting alone will do little to address bullying without appropriate investigation of complaints, issuing of reasonable consequences for children who bully, and provision of supports for children who are bullied (Limber & Small, 2003). Model policy provisions related to investigation, disciplinary actions, and interventions for children who are bullied are examined next.

Step 4: Clarify Investigation and Disciplinary Actions

Massachusetts' sample policy (Mass. Gov., n.d.) describes a very detailed process for resolving complaints through informal and formal proceedings. Other model/sample policies include brief, clear statements of responsibilities of school staff to accept and investigate reports. Vermont's policy (Vermont Department of Education, n.d.), for example, requires designated school officials to

> accept and review all reports of bullying, including anonymous reports. If after initial inquiry, an anonymous or oral report appears to warrant further investigation, school districts shall promptly continue with an investigation. (p. 2)

Almost all sample/model policies note that schools may take disciplinary action against students who bully and that the particular action taken will depend on characteristics of the student(s) involved and the situation. Maine's sample policy (Maine School Management Association, n.d.), for example, acknowledges that

> in determining the appropriate response to students who engage in bullying behavior, school administrators should consider the ages and maturity of the students involved, the type of behaviors, the frequency and/or pattern of behaviors, the context in which the incident occurred, and other relevant circumstances. Consequences may range from positive behavioral interventions up to and including suspension, expulsion, and/or reports to law enforcement officials. (p. 3)

Step 5: Include Assistance for Victims of Bullying

Within states' model/sample policies, alarmingly little attention has been paid to providing support for victims of bullying. We found mention of such support in only a small minority of the policies that we reviewed. Rhode Island's sample policy (n.d.) mentions that

> if the victim's mental health has been placed at risk appropriate referrals will be made. If the bullying included a violent criminal offense the victim of the bullying will be informed [of] any school transfer rights he or she may have under the Federal No Child Left Behind Act (NCLB, 2001). (p. 6)

Colorado's Association of School Boards (Center for the Study and Prevention of Violence, n.d.) sample policy requires each superintendent to develop a comprehensive program to address bullying, which should be geared toward accomplishing a variety of goals, including "[supporting] victims of bullying by means of individual and peer counseling."

As researchers continue to document negative emotional, physical, and academic consequences of bullying (see Limber, 2006, for a review), local policymakers are encouraged to include language in their local bullying policies that direct staff to assess victims of bullying for potential problems that may have resulted from the bullying and to provide support and/or referrals as warranted.

Step 6: Include Training and Prevention Procedures

Although most state model/sample policies address the need for training and/or other prevention strategies, they vary in their focus and level of specificity. California's sample policy (n.d.) simply notes that the district "will provide staff development training in bullying prevention . . . to build each school's capacity to maintain a safe and healthy learning environment."

At least two model/sample policies (Colorado and New Jersey) require or encourage comprehensive approaches to bullying prevention. For example, under Colorado's Association of School Boards (Center for the Study and Prevention of Violence) model policy:

> the superintendent shall develop a comprehensive program at all school levels that is aimed at accomplishing a variety of goals, including to train staff and students in taking pro-active steps to prevent bullying from occurring . . . to foster a productive partnership with parents and community members in order to help maintain a bully-free environment . . . to help develop peer support networks . . . [and] to recognize and praise positive, supportive behaviors of students toward one another on a regular basis.

Similarly, New Jersey's model policy (State of New Jersey, Department of Education, 2007) encourages both individual and "institutional" responses to bullying, noting that "institutional . . . responses can range from school and community surveys . . . to focus groups, to adoption of research-based bullying prevention program models, to training . . . to participation of parents and other community members and organizations" (p. 11). In its commentary accompanying the model policy, New Jersey administrators encourage districts to establish a range of responses to bullying, "including individual, classroom, school or district level responses, as appropriate" (p. 12).

Unfortunately, in some sample/model policies, descriptions of efforts to prevent bullying are completely absent. In most others, preventive efforts are given very short shrift, as policy language focuses primarily on the prohibition of bullying and on reporting procedures and sanctions. As suggested earlier, school-based efforts that focus exclusively on reporting and individual interventions are unlikely to be effective (see Limber & Small, 2003). As part of its National Bullying Prevention Campaign, the Health Resources and Services Administration (n.d.) highlighted 10 elements of best practice to address bullying in schools (see adapted version of this list in Figure 4.1), which included a focus on changing the social norms of the whole school environment, assessment, training of all staff, development of a team to coordinate the school's efforts, staff and parent involvement, clear rules and consequences for engaging in and/or supporting bullying, increased adult supervision, consistent individual interventions for involved students, classroom time to focus on bullying and peer relations, and continuing efforts over time (Health Resources and Services Administration, n.d.). Although we fully recognize the limited funding options available to many schools, we nevertheless strongly encourage adoption of local policies that have, at their core, a recognition of the importance of research-based comprehensive prevention efforts. We also encourage ongoing evaluation of these local efforts. Two sample policies (Iowa and Maine) stipulate periodic evaluation of the prevention, intervention, and training efforts in the school district, and we encourage local policymakers to follow their examples.

POLICY IMPLEMENTATION

State mandates are necessary in many respects in order to "force" school districts to develop an anti-bullying policy. However, effective implementation of policies can be difficult. Keeping in mind the 80/20 principle (Koch, 1998), we know that if we don't have 80% buy-in from teachers, parents, administrators, and students for a particular program, the likelihood of that program being successful is minimal. Thus, schools need to have strong administrative and staff support for anti-bullying policies and procedures. The first step in policy implementation is to identify an anti-bullying task force whose members include key school and community stakeholders. Ideally, the task force would also include members who were on the committee that developed the anti-bullying policy for the district. Policies need to be accessible, and the school needs to make copies of their policies available for public review. School administrators and school staff need to know what their policies state. As mentioned earlier in this chapter, 50% of professional staff at a staff development workshop did not know whether their school had an anti-bullying policy. Staff development training including a review of school policies and procedures should occur on a yearly basis. Key elements of anti-bullying policies should be adopted in all classrooms, and these policies should support classroom policies and procedures. Ideally, anti-bullying policies should provide a common language and set of procedures for effectively intervening in bullying behaviors and should be communicated across school personnel, students, and parents. Effective policy develop-

Change the school climate

 Assess bullying/victimization

 Train ALL staff

 Create an anti-bullying advisory team

 Actively include staff, parents, and students

 Disseminate clear rules and consequences

 Increase adult supervision

 Provide consistent individual intervention

 Allow class time to focus on social emotional learning

 Continue these efforts annually

FIGURE 4.1. Top 10 best policy practices for schools.

ment and implementation can set the stage for permanent reduction of bullying behaviors in our nation's schools.

CONCLUSIONS AND RECOMMENDATIONS

We firmly believe that all schools should create, adopt, and annually monitor anti-bullying policies. Unfortunately, unless mandated by state or federal law, many school districts will not create, adopt, or enforce anti-bullying policies. We have noted that the attention historically given to discrimination, harassment, and use of weapons has dramatically affected policies and practices around these issues. It is our observation and experience that the same trend is happening with bullying. Thus, it is our hope that bullying will receive the same attention that has been given to these other important societal conflicts.

While bullying is a significant problem in our schools and communities, we also discussed the fact that zero tolerance and punishment-based strategies are not effective for reducing bullying behaviors. In the next chapter, we will discuss the legal issues involved in bullying/victimization.

CASE EXAMPLE:
KEVIN—HEAR NO EVIL, SEE NO EVIL, SPEAK NO EVIL

Kevin was a very shy preadolescent when his parents brought him to treatment. The initial referral question related to anxiety and depression. Indeed, Kevin was diagnosed with depression and social anxiety. However, as Kevin continued in therapy, it became apparent that he was having problems with bullying.

Kevin related a recent experience in which he was walking home from school and another student threatened to beat him up. This had happened many times before, but this time the other student chased Kevin for several blocks and threw rocks at him. Kevin was not physically hurt, but he was shaken up. To make matters worse, this other kid was in several of Kevin's classes. Kevin came home and told his mother about what had happened and stated that he was afraid to go to school the next day.

Kevin's mother reassured him it would be fine and that she would talk with the principal the following day. Before school, Kevin's mother went in and met with the principal. Much to her surprise, the principal told her that there was nothing the school could do since the incident happened off of school grounds and the school had a policy that they could only respond to incidents that happen on school property. Kevin's mother was confused and upset. This student would be in class with her son that day. She insisted that the other student be moved a fair distance from her son if they were going to be in the same class and that the teacher be alerted to the situation. Reluctantly, the principal agreed, and Kevin was comfortable enough to return to class.

Thoughts about Kevin's Case

This case highlights the importance of parents acting as advocates for their children. All schools have policies for student behavior; however, not all parents know their school's policies. Administrators are often hesitant to intervene, especially when the bullying incident occurred off of school grounds. However, school personnel have an obligation to create a safe environment for all students once they are in the school building. Events occurring out of school are relevant to a child's feelings of safety in school.

FOLLOW-UP QUESTIONS

1. Does your school have an anti-bullying policy? Have you read it? Do you know what it mandates?

2. If your school has an anti-bullying policy, does it guide your behavior? Do you use it in your classroom?

3. Do the students in your school (or classroom) know what the anti-bullying policy is? How can policies be effectively used to intervene and shape student behavior?

4. Many students like Kevin who are bullied off school grounds tell us that they're afraid to go to school because the students who are doing the bullying are in their school. What dilemma does this pose for school administrators? For students? For parents? Should anti-bullying policies include statements about where bullying occurs? If so, what about cyberbullying?

5

Legal Issues for School Personnel

REBECCA ALLEY *and* SUSAN P. LIMBER

Bullying among American schoolchildren has existed since students first gathered in one-room school houses, and many educators, parents, and children have quietly struggled with this problem over the years. Attention to bullying by policymakers and the public, however, is a very recent phenomenon. In the years after the tragic shootings at Columbine High School, the issue of bullying exploded in the news media. Research on the topic also increased dramatically, and numerous bullying programs and resources have been published for use in schools. In addition, a recent flurry of state legislation related to bullying and a number of highly publicized lawsuits have raised concerns among educators about their legal options and responsibilities to prevent and address bullying in their schools.

In this chapter, we trace the development of bullying laws in the United States and summarize current statutory provisions. Because most state laws require the development of local school district policies on bullying (and a number of state departments of education have provided model policies for local school officials to follow), we refer to the common elements of these policies as described in Chapter 4. We also review recent litigation related to bullying, including claims brought against schools, school districts, and individual employees under federal laws as well as those brought under state law. We end with a case example of a young girl who committed suicide as a result of significant bullying and explore the reasons why her parents chose not to litigate.

STATE LAWS ABOUT BULLYING

Although federal laws governing students and schools do exist in the United States, the daily operations of our nation's public schools are regulated primarily at the state and local levels. State legislatures, in particular, have a great deal of power to dictate the rights and responsibilities of students, teachers, and school administrators, and, through state statutes, they provide general guidelines for school and district policies on a wide range of educational issues, including bullying.

Before the last decade, state statutes addressing bullying in schools were nonexistent in this country. It was not until 1999 that the Georgia legislature, spurred by a highly publicized bullying incident resulting in the death of a middle school student, enacted the first state statute to specifically address bullying in schools. Other state legislatures soon followed suit, some prompted by similar incidents of violence in their own states. By far the most notorious of these incidents were the school shootings at Columbine High School near Littleton, Colorado, on April 20, 1999. That morning two teenage boys went on a shooting rampage at their school, killing 12 students and a teacher and wounding 24 others before committing suicide. In the aftermath of the shootings, evidence that the two boys had been bullied at school and that this may have contributed to their actions drew significant national attention to the problem of school bullying. This new national awareness about the dangers of bullying prompted not just the Colorado state legislature but other state legislatures as well to pass anti-bullying legislation over the next several years.

Currently, 33 states have anti-bullying laws in place, and at least 10 others are considering passing similar laws (see Table 5.1 for a full listing of laws and citations).[1] Although these statutes vary in their specifics, all mandate that state or local officials establish policies against student bullying of other students in state public schools. The majority of the 33 states require anti-bullying policies at the district level, although four states (California, Indiana, Maine, and Vermont) require individual schools to create their own policies and two others (Maryland and Nevada) leave the job of establishing anti-bullying policies to the state department of education. For a state-by-state guide to anti-bullying legislation, see Table 5.2 and also consider checking each state's website for the most current information.

DEFINITIONS

To understand the substance and scope of any law, it is necessary to understand the key terminology; thus, in the case of anti-bullying legislation, determining what is meant by "bullying" is essential to a true comprehension and appropriate application of the law. Of the 33 states with anti-bullying laws, only 22 expressly define bullying. Two states, Maryland

---

[1]These numbers are provided as of July 16, 2008.

TABLE 5.1. Listing of Bullying Statutes by State

Alaska	2006 Alaska Sess. Laws 109
Arizona	*Arizona Revised Statute* § 15-341 (2005)
Arkansas	*Arkansas Code Annotated* § 6-18-514 (Michie 2006) *Arkansas Code Annotated* § 6-18-1005 (Michie 2006)
California	*California Education Code* § 32261 (Deering 2006) *California Education Code* § 32265 (Deering 2006) *California Education Code* § 32270 (Deering 2006) *California Education Code* § 35294.21 (Deering 2006)
Colorado	*Colorado Revised Statute* § 22-32-109.1 (2005)
Connecticut	*2006 Connecticut Public Acts* 115
Delaware	*Delaware Code Annotated title* 14, § 4112D (2007) *Delaware Code Annotated title* 14, § 4123A (2007)
Georgia	*Georgia Code Annotated* § 20-2-751.4 (2006) *Georgia Code Annotated* § 20-2-145 (2006) *Georgia Code Annotated* § 20-2-751.5 (2006)
Idaho	*Idaho Code Annotated* § 33-205 (2006) *Idaho Code Annotated* § 33-512 (2006) *Idaho Code Annotated* § 18-917A (2006)
Illinois	*105 Illinois Compiled Statute* 5/10-20.14 (2006) *105 Illinois Compiled Statute* 5/27-23.7 (2006)
Indiana	*Indiana Code Annotated* § 5-2-10.1-2 (Michie 2006) *Indiana Code Annotated* § 5-2-10.1-11 (Michie 2006) *Indiana Code Annotated* § 5-2-10.1-12 (Michie 2006) *Indiana Code Annotated* § 20-33-8-0.2 (Michie 2006) *Indiana Code Annotated* § 20-33-8-13.5 (Michie 2006)
Iowa	*Iowa Code* § 280.28 (2007)
Kansas	*Kansas Statute Annotated* § 72-6433 (2007)
Louisiana	*Louisiana Revised Statute Annotated* § 17:416.13 (2006) *Louisiana Revised Statute Annotated* § 17:416.17 (2006)
Maine	*Maine Revised Statute Annotated* 20-A, § 1001 (2006)
Maryland	Safe Schools Reporting Act of 2005, *Maryland Code Annotated Education* § 7-424 (2006)
Minnesota	*Minnesota Statute* § 121A.0695 (2005)
Missouri	2006 Mo. SB 894
Nevada	*Nevada Revised Statute Annotated* 388.125 (Michie 2006) *Nevada Revised Statute Annotated* 388.132 (Michie 2006) *Nevada Revised Statute Annotated* 388.133 (Michie 2006) *Nevada Revised Statute Annotated* 388.134 (Michie 2006)

(continued)

TABLE 5.1. *(continued)*

Nevada *(cont.)*	*Nevada Revised Statute Annotated* 388.135 (Michie 2006) *Nevada Revised Statute Annotated* 388.136 (Michie 2006) *Nevada Revised Statute Annotated* 388.137 (Michie 2006) *Nevada Revised Statute Annotated* 388.139 (Michie 2006) *Nevada Revised Statute Annotated* 388.1345 (Michie 2006)
New Hampshire	Pupil Safety and Violence Prevention Act, *New Hampshire Revised Statute Annotated* § 193-F:2 (2006) *New Hampshire Revised Statute Annotated* § 193-F:3 (2006)
New Jersey	*New Jersey Statute Annotated* § 18A:37-13 to 17 (2006)
New York	Project SAVE, Safe Schools Against Violence in Education Act, *New York Education Law* § 2801-a (Consol. 2006)
Ohio	*Ohio Revised Code Annotated* § 3301.22 (LexisNexis 2007) *Ohio Revised Code Annotated* § 3313.666 (LexisNexis 2007) *Ohio Revised Code Annotated* § 3313.667 (LexisNexis 2007)
Oklahoma	School Bullying Prevention Act, *Oklahoma Statute* 70, § 24-100.2 to 100. 5 (2005)
Oregon	*Oregon Revised Statute* § 339.351 (2006) *Oregon Revised Statute* § 339.353 (2006) *Oregon Revised Statute* § 339.356 (2006) *Oregon Revised Statute* § 339.359 (2006) *Oregon Revised Statute* § 339.362 (2006) *Oregon Revised Statute* § 339.364 (2006)
Rhode Island	*Rhode Island General Laws* § 16-21-24 (2006) *Rhode Island General Laws* § 16-21-26 (2006)
South Carolina	Safe School Climate Act, 2006 South Carolina Acts 353
Tennessee	*Tennessee Code Annotated* § 49-6-1014 to 1019 (2005)
Texas	*Texas Education Code Annotated* § 25.0341 (Vernon 2006) *Texas Education Code Annotated* § 37.001 (Vernon 2006) *Texas Education Code Annotated* § 37.083 (Vernon 2006)
Vermont	*Vermont Statute Annotated* 16, § 11 (2006) *Vermont Statute Annotated* 16, § 165 (2006) *Vermont Statute Annotated* 16, § 565 (2006) *Vermont Statute Annotated* 16, § 1161a (2006)
Virginia	*Virginia Code Annotated* § 8.01-220.1:2 (Michie 2006) *Virginia Code Annotated* § 22.1-208.01 (Michie 2006) *Virginia Code Annotated* § 22.1-279.6 (Michie 2006)
Washington	*Washington Revised Code* § 28A.300.285 (2006) *Washington Revised Code* § 28A. 600.480 (2006)
West Virginia	*West Virginia Code Annotated* § 18-2C-1 to 6 (Michie 2006)

Note. These citations are current as of July 16, 2008.

TABLE 5.2. Anti-Bullying Laws by State

State	Who is responsible for creating anti-bullying policy	Definition of bullying	Policy requirements or recommendations[a]	Model policy required
Alaska	School district	✓	• Reporting requirement for employees and students • Recording process • Disciplinary procedures	✓
Arizona	School district		• Reporting requirement for employees • Investigation requirement • Recording process • Disciplinary procedures	
Arkansas	School district		• Reporting requirement for employees • Disciplinary procedures	
California	School			
Colorado	School district	✓	• Recording process	
Connecticut	School district	✓	• Reporting requirement for employees • Investigation requirement • Parental notification requirement • Recording process • Intervention procedures	
Delaware	School district	✓	• Reporting requirement for employees • Investigation requirement • Disciplinary procedures • Parental notification requirement	✓
Georgia	School district	✓	• Parental notification requirement • Disciplinary procedures	
Idaho	School district	✓		
Illinois	School district		• Parental notification requirement • Intervention procedures	
Indiana	School	✓	• Reporting requirement • Investigation requirement • Parental involvement requirement • Intervention procedures	
Iowa	School district	✓	• Disciplinary procedures • Reporting procedure • Investigation procedure • Recording process	

TABLE 5.2. *(continued)*

State	Who is responsible for creating anti-bullying policy	Definition of bullying	Policy requirements or recommendations[a]	Model policy required
Kansas	School district	✓		
Louisiana	School district	✓		
Maine	School			✓
Maryland	State		• Reporting procedure • Recording process	
Minnesota	School district			
Missouri	School district	✓	• Reporting requirement for employees • Disciplinary procedures	
Nevada	State		• Reporting requirement • Recording process	
New Hampshire	School district		• Reporting requirement for employees • Parental notification requirement • Recording process	
New Jersey	School district	✓	• Reporting procedure • Investigation procedure • Disciplinary procedures	✓
New York	School district			
Ohio	School district	✓	• Reporting procedure • Reporting requirement for employees • Parental notification requirement • Recording process • Investigation procedure • Disciplinary procedure	✓
Oklahoma	School district	✓	• Disciplinary procedures	
Oregon	School district	✓	• (Reporting procedure) • (Investigation procedure) • (Disciplinary procedures)	
Rhode Island	School district	✓	• Reporting provision	✓

(continued)

TABLE 5.2. *(continued)*

State	Who is responsible for creating anti-bullying policy	Definition of bullying	Policy requirements or recommendations[a]	Model policy required
South Carolina	School district	✓	• Reporting requirement for employees and students • Investigation procedure • Disciplinary procedures	✓
Tennessee	School district	✓	• (Reporting procedure) • (Investigation procedure) • (Disciplinary procedures)	
Texas	School district	✓		
Vermont	School	✓		✓
Virginia	School district			✓
Washington	School district	✓		✓
West Virginia	School district	✓	• Reporting requirement for employees • Investigation procedure • Parental notification requirement • Recording process • Disciplinary procedures	✓

[a]Recommended provisions are indicated in parentheses.

and Nevada, do not use the term "bullying" explicitly but rather require policies against student-on-student "harassment," a term that both states define. The remaining nine states (Arizona, Arkansas, California, Illinois, Maine, Minnesota, New Hampshire, New York, and Virginia) require policies against bullying without defining the parameters of bullying behavior. By doing so, these states' statutes leave local school and district administrators to guess what behaviors may be included in anti-bullying laws.

Researchers and practitioners typically define bullying as aggressive behavior that is intentional, is repeated over time, and involves an imbalance of power or strength (Nansel et al., 2001; Olweus, 1993a; Stop Bullying Now, n.d.). Among the 22 state definitions of bullying, there is wide variability in the degree to which they comport with this definition and with each other. For instance, 14 states limit bullying to intentional acts on the part of the child who bullies. For example, the State of Washington's definition refers to "any intentional, verbal, or physical act . . . . [which] physically harms a student or damages the student's property . . . . or . . . . has the effect of substantially interfering with a student's education . . . . or . . . . is so severe, persistent, or pervasive that it creates an intimidating or threatening educational environment . . . . or . . . . has the effect of substantially disrupting the orderly operation of the school" (*Washington Revised Code*, 2006). Two states (Connecticut and Vermont) limit their definitions of bullying to acts that are repeated over time, and one state (Georgia) even limits its definition to acts of a physical nature. Additionally, six states specify the locations where bullying may occur. Colorado, for example, maintains that bullying includes acts taken "in the school, on school grounds, in school vehicles, at a designated school bus stop, or at school activities or sanctioned events" (Colorado Revised Statutes, 2005).

Perhaps the most problematic statutory definitions belong to those 11 states (Alaska, Iowa, Louisiana, New Jersey, Ohio, Oklahoma, Oregon, Rhode Island, South Carolina, Washington, and West Virginia) that define bullying as synonymous with harassment and intimidation. For example, Oklahoma's anti-bullying statute states that

> as used in the School Bullying Prevention Act . . . "harassment, intimidation, and bullying" mean any gesture, written or verbal expression, or physical act that a reasonable person should know will harm another student, damage another student's property, place another student in reasonable fear of harm to the student's person or damage to the student's property, or insult or demean any student or group of students in such a way as to disrupt or interfere with the school's educational mission or the education of any student. (School Bullying Prevention Act, 2005)

In contrast to the definition of bullying just provided, harassment involves discriminatory behavior toward protected classes of individuals (Limber & Small, 2003). That is, whereas children who bully may act aggressively toward their victim for any reason, or for no reason at all, perpetrators of harassment act in a discriminatory manner based on some characteristic of the victim.

Although legal prohibitions against bullying in schools are relatively new, prohibitions against student harassment based on race, religion, national origin, gender, or disability are well established in our nation's law. Moreover, prohibitions against harassment exist at both the state and federal levels, in contrast to the new wave of bullying legislation, which so far exists solely at the state level. Federal law requires schools to prohibit certain types of harassment, such as harassment based on race, gender, or disability, in order to receive federal funds (e.g., Title VI of the Civil Rights Act of 1964, which prohibits discrimination based on race; Title IX of the Education Amendment Act of 1972, which prohibits discrimination based on gender; and Section 504 of the Rehabilitation Act of 1973, which prohibits discrimination based on disability), and the U.S. Supreme Court has itself implied that federal law governing harassment behavior does not apply to bullying (see *Davis v. Monroe County Board of Education*, 1999). (The Court in *Davis* noted, "In the school setting, students often engage in insults, banter, teasing, shoving, pushing, and gender-specific conduct that is upsetting to the students subjected to it. Damages are not available for simple acts of teasing and name-calling among school children, however."[2]) Thus, by providing a single definition for "bullying, harassment, and intimidation," states such as Oklahoma muddle

---

[2]One might, of course, quarrel with the Court's depiction of these and other bullying behaviors as "simple acts."

the important practical and legal distinctions between the terms. The significance of these distinctions for school administrators seeking to avoid liability for bullying and harassment in their schools is discussed in greater detail in the "Litigation" section of this chapter.

POLICY REQUIREMENTS AND RECOMMENDATIONS

Providing definitions of bullying and harassment are not the only way, however, that state legislatures have sought to aid local school officials in crafting anti-bullying policies. For instance, 20 state statutes list specific policy requirements, such as disciplinary and reporting procedures, which schools or districts must include in their anti-bullying policies. Three other states (Oregon, Tennessee, and Washington) provide specific policy recommendations, which, although not required by law, give schools and districts a certain amount of guidance in creating their policies. This leaves 10 states (California, Idaho, Kansas, Louisiana, Maine, Minnesota, New York, Texas, Vermont, and Virginia), however, whose legislatures have required schools or districts to set up anti-bullying policies but have failed to provide any specific requirements or recommendations for those policies.

Reporting of Incidents

Among the 23 states providing specific policy requirements or recommendations, 18 require or recommend procedures for reporting of bullying incidents. Of those 18 states, 10 (Alaska, Arizona, Arkansas, Connecticut, Delaware, Missouri, New Hampshire, Ohio, South Carolina, and West Virginia) either directly require that school or district employees report incidents of bullying or require that school bullying policies include procedures for such reporting. For example, Alaska requires that "a school employee, student, or volunteer who has witnessed, or has reliable information that a student has been subjected to harassment, intimidation, or bullying, whether verbal or physical, shall report the incident to an appropriate school official" (Alaska Session Laws, 2006). Four of those states (Alaska, Arizona, Connecticut, and South Carolina) similarly mandate provisions for student reporting. For example, Arizona requires district anti-bullying policies to include "a procedure for pupils to confidentially report to school officials incidents of harassment, intimidation or bullying" (*Arizona Revised Statutes*, 2005).

Immunity

Interestingly, 18 states provide some version of an immunity clause, purporting to grant immunity to school employees or others who report incidents of bullying to the appropriate authorities in good faith. For example, West Virginia's anti-bullying statute states that "a school employee, student or volunteer is individually immune from a cause of action for damages arising from reporting said incident, if that person: (1) in good faith promptly reports an incident of harassment, intimidation or bullying; (2) makes the report to the appropriate school official as designated by policy; and (3) makes the report in compliance with the procedures as specified in policy" (*West Virginia Code Annotated*, 2006a). Although such provisions may seem to suggest to school employees that they may avoid civil liability for incidents of bullying simply by reporting the incidents under their school or district anti-bullying policy, this is an incorrect assumption. Even if a state's immunity provision were to allow an employee to avoid liability under state law, an immunity provision in a state statute has no effect on that employee's liability under federal law. Furthermore, most state constitutions provide their own limitations on the extent to which state statutes may provide immunity to state employees. To the extent that an immunity provision in a state anti-bullying provision is in conflict with one or more provisions of that state's constitution, the statute is invalid. Simply put, school and district employees should be aware that the immunity purportedly provided in some anti-bullying statutes is by no means absolute and is subject to limitations of both state and federal laws.

Investigation

In addition to reporting requirements, 11 states (Arizona, Connecticut, Delaware, Indiana, Iowa, New Jersey, Ohio, Oregon, South Carolina, Tennessee, and West Virginia) require or recommend provisions for the investigation of bullying incidents, and 11 (Alaska, Arizona, Colorado, Connecticut, Delaware, Iowa, Maryland, Nevada, New Hampshire, Ohio, and West Virginia) require reporting or documentation of bullying incidents. Connecticut, for example, requires "each school to maintain a list of the number of verified acts of bullying in such school and make such list available for public inspection" (*Connecticut Public Acts*, 2006). Additionally, 16 states require or recommend that bullying policies contain provisions setting forth disciplinary or intervention procedures. For example, Tennessee encourages school districts to include "a statement of the consequences and appropriate remedial action for a person who commits an act of harassment, intimidation or bullying" in their anti-bullying policies (*Tennessee Code Annotated*, 2005).

Notification

In comparison to other policy requirements and recommendations, relatively few states— only seven—require schools to notify parents when children are involved in bullying incidents in school. Of those seven states, three (New Hampshire, Ohio, and West Virginia) require school officials to inform parents of all children involved; New Hampshire even goes so far as to specifically require that the school principal must report all incidents to parents within 48 hours both by telephone and in writing. Connecticut and Delaware similarly require notification of parents of the perpetrators and victims, whereas Illinois mandates parental notification without specifying which parents must be notified. Finally, Georgia requires notification only of parents of perpetrators and only when the incident occurs on a school bus. Related to these parental notification requirements, a sixth state, Indiana, mandates that "discipline rules adopted by the governing body of a school corporation . . . prohibit bullying . . . and . . . include provisions concerning education, parental involvement, reporting, investigation, and intervention." Thus, the Indiana statute requires bullying policies to contain a "parental involvement" provision, as well as other mentioned provisions, but fails to provide any details regarding what such a provision should look like.

Disciplinary Procedures for Children Who Bully

Seventeen state statutes highlight the importance of disciplining children who bully their peers. Most, however, do not prescribe particular disciplinary actions. Under New Jersey law, for example, local bullying policies must include the "consequences and appropriate remedial actions for a person who commits an act of harassment, intimidation or bullying" (*New Jersey Statutes Annotated*, 2006). By far the most punitive statute belongs to Georgia, which directs local school boards to require that "upon a finding that a student [in grades 6–12] has committed the offense of bullying for the third time in a school year, such student shall be assigned to an alternative school" (*Georgia Code Annotated*, 2006).

Training and Prevention

In addition to the aforementioned requirements and recommendations for anti-bullying policies, 15 states require or provide guidelines for employee training on bullying prevention and relevant anti-bullying policies. Among these 15 states, the nature and extent of provisions regarding bullying training and prevention vary. For instance, Missouri's statute simply states that "the district [anti-bullying] policy shall address training of employees in the requirements of the district policy" (Mo. SB 894, 2006). In contrast, West Virginia recommends, rather than requires, such training, stating that "schools and county boards are encouraged, but not required, to form bullying prevention taskforces, programs and other initiatives involving school staff, students,

teachers, administrators, volunteers, parents, law enforcement and community members" (*West Virginia Code Annotated*, 2006b). The West Virginia statute also mandates, however, that "information regarding the county board policy against harassment, intimidation or bullying shall be incorporated into each school's current employee training program" (*West Virginia Code Annotated*, 2006b). Additionally, some states set aside funds for training and prevention purpose. For example, Indiana has created a "safe schools fund" to, among other things, "provide educational outreach and training to school personnel concerning . . . the identification of, . . . the prevention of, . . . and . . . intervention in . . . bullying" (*Indiana Code Annotated*, 2006).

Model Policies

In order to guide schools and school districts in establishing anti-bullying policies, 11 state statutes currently require state departments of education to develop model policies. These model policies are described in detail in Chapter 4.

LITIGATION

Legal interest in bullying has not been limited to actions by state legislatures. In recent years, there has been much speculation about perceived increases in the number of law-suits (and the number of successful lawsuits) related to bullying incidents (e.g., Seper, 2005). Although the news media's coverage of the shootings at Columbine and other incidents of school violence have certainly drawn increased attention to bullying, actual increases and trends in litigation are difficult to measure for several reasons. First, many, if not most, law-suits of this type are settled out of court, meaning that court records of such litigation are scarce and by no means comprehensive. For instance, as part of the settlement agreement, the parties may agree to keep the settlement amount private. Although such nondisclosure agreements may be particularly attractive to defendant school districts that are fearful that large settlement amounts will encourage further lawsuits, they also make tracking trends in litigation more difficult. Second, there is no national system for counting and tracking the lawsuits related to incidents of school violence that do make it to court. Thus, although officials at the local level may report increases in such litigation, trends at the national level are difficult to determine. Third, the primary legal databases on which lawyers and legal scholars rely include only court decisions that made on appeal. This means that cases that are decided at the trial court level and do not reach an appeals court are not represented in these databases. Presumably, these databases are, therefore, skewed to overrepresent the "close" cases and underrepresent the "easy" cases, which are more likely to be settled out of court or not reach appeal.

That said, some large settlement and court awards in the last several years have raised concerns among school employees and administrators about the costs of bullying litigation. In 2004, the Tonganoxie School District in Kansas paid $440,000 to settle a lawsuit brought by high school student who left his school after he was bullied by his classmates because they thought he was gay (*WIBW.com*, 2005). That same year, a $4.5 million settlement was agreed to between the Anchorage School District in Alaska and the family of a middle school student who tried to commit suicide after he was bullied at school (Pesznecker, 2004). In 2005, a New Jersey appellate court upheld a jury award for $50,000 to a high school student who was physically and verbally abused by his peers on the basis of his perceived sexual orientation (Mikle, 2005). To avoid these types of results, school professionals should first be aware of the different types of lawsuits that may be brought against them in connection with bullying incidents.

Litigants—those individuals bringing a lawsuit (typically the victim of bullying or the parents of the victim)—may bring lawsuits in either federal or state court. Which court will depend on whether the litigants have any claims under federal law, in which case they may bring their lawsuit in federal court, or whether their claims are limited to those under state law, in which case they must bring their lawsuit in state court. The litigants, also known as plaintiffs, may combine several legal claims into a single lawsuit. In fact, such combining of claims is quite common in litigation involving school bullying. For example, in one Massachusetts case, a victim of bullying and her parents sued the town, school district, and bullies under the Rehabilitation Act, Title IX, and Section 1983 as well as Massachusetts' state law against the intentional infliction of emotional distress (*Doe v. Town of Bourne*, 2004). Additionally, litigants bringing suits for damages based on bullying incidents can, and have, brought their suits against a number of different defendants, including the school, school district, various school officials, and district employees as well as against children who bully and their parents (*Ray v. Antioch Unified School District*, 2000; *Snelling v. Fall Mountain Regional School District*, 2001; *Theno v. Tonganoxie Unified School District No. 464*, 2005).

CLAIMS UNDER FEDERAL LAW

Although there is currently no federal law against bullying per se, victims of bullying and their parents may seek damages under a number of federal laws that prohibit harassment against protected classes of individuals. For example, although a student who is repeatedly taunted and beaten up at school because of his race cannot bring a federal lawsuit based on the fact that he was bullied, he can, under certain circumstances, make a claim for damages under Title VI of the Civil Rights Act of 1964, which prohibits harassment based on race. The federal laws that are most often implicated in lawsuits based on incidents of school bullying relate either to gender, race, or disability harassment or to a deprivation of a student's federally protected rights. These laws and their relation to bullying are discussed in turn next.

Claims against Schools and School Districts

Claims against schools and school districts may be based on sexual or gender-based harassment, racial harassment, and disability harassment.

Claims Based on Sexual or Gender-Based Harassment

Claims based on sexual harassment or gender discrimination typically rely on Title IX of the Education Act Amendments of 1972. This federal statute, commonly referred to simply as Title IX, states that "no person in the United States shall, on the basis of sex, be excluded from participation in, be denied the benefits of, or be subjected to discrimination under any education program or activity receiving Federal financial assistance" (Education Amendment Acts of 1972, 2006). In the seminal case of *Davis v. Monroe County Board of Education*, the U.S. Supreme Court expressly held that, under Title IX, schools and districts may be liable for student-on-student sexual harassment in certain situations. Specifically, the

Davis Court held that a school or district may be liable for peer sexual harassment under Title IX when the school or district acted with "deliberate indifference" toward harassment that was "so severe, pervasive, and objectively offensive that it denies its victims the equal access to education that Title IX is designed to protect."

This ruling establishes several high hurdles for litigants in subsequent cases. First, to find that a defendant school or district acted with "deliberate indifference," a court must find that the defendant had actual knowledge of the harassment and that its response was "clearly unreasonable in light of the known circumstances." Second, the harassment itself must rise to a certain level. In this regard, the *Davis* Court specifically noted:

> It is not enough to show . . . that a student has been "teased," or "called . . . offensive names[.]" Comparisons to an "overweight child who skips gym class because the other children tease her about her size," the student "who refuses to wear glasses to avoid the taunts of 'four-eyes,'" and "the child who refuses to go to school because the school bully calls him a 'scardy-cat' at recess," are inapposite and misleading [citations omitted]. (*Davis v. Monroe County Board of Education*, 1999)

Finally, the Court stressed that the impact on the student's access to education must be significant, as evidenced by more than "a mere decline in grades."

In addition to setting these high hurdles for litigants in peer sexual harassment cases, the *Davis* decision clearly limited the number of potential defendants against whom Title IX claims might be brought. That is, the Court maintained that claims under Title IX may only be brought against recipients of federal funds, such as schools and school districts, and not against individuals, such as school teachers or administrators. Practically, this limitation creates yet another high hurdle for many litigants, who, although they can show that particular teachers, coaches, or school employees knew of the harassment in question, may not have sufficient evidence to show knowledge at the school or district level. Moreover, who must have knowledge of bullying within a school or district (e.g., vice principal, principal, superintendent) and what constitutes knowledge may vary from state to state and even judge to judge.

Overall, the *Davis* decision is central to an understanding of federal harassment law not only because it sets forth the standard for schools' liability in peer sexual harassment cases, but also because courts often apply the standard set forth in *Davis* to claims based on other types of peer harassment (e.g., peer harassment based on race, gender, or disability). For instance, there are two other contexts besides peer sexual harassment in which victims of peer harassment may invoke Title IX. The first involves nonsexual harassment of female students based on their gender by either male or female peers (e.g., gender-based name calling). The second involves harassment of male or female students based on their "failure to meet gender stereotypes" (e.g., a male student who exhibits effeminate characteristics or participates in traditionally female activities) or their perceived or actual sexual orientation. Many courts have declined to interpret Title IX as prohibiting the latter type of harassment and have dismissed Title IX claims based on sexual orientation harassment for this reason. Where courts have considered such claims, however, they typically apply the *Davis* standard.

Claims Based on Racial Harassment

Title VI of the Civil Rights Act of 1964 provides that "no person in the United States shall, on the ground of race, color, or national origin, be excluded from participation in, be denied the benefits of, or be subjected to discrimination under any program or activity receiving Federal financial assistance." Although Title VI claims are based on a different federal law than Title IX claims, courts typically apply the *Davis* standard to determine a school or district's liability for student-on-student harassment based on the victim's race or national origin (see *Curley v. Hill*, 2000). That is, in order to collect monetary damages from a school or district for peer racial harassment under Title VI a litigant must show that the defendant school or district acted with deliberate indifference toward harassment that is so severe, pervasive, and objectively offensive as to deprive the victim of access to educational opportunities.

Claims Based on Disability Harassment

Several federal statutes may be implicated in claims for peer harassment based on the physical or mental disability of the victim. These include Section 504 of the Rehabilitation Act of 1973 and Title II of the Americans with Disabilities Act (ADA). Section 504 of the Rehabilitation Act of 1973 states that "no otherwise qualified individual with a disability in the United States . . . shall, solely by reason of her or his disability, be excluded from the participation in, be denied the benefits of, or be subjected to discrimination under any program or activity receiving Federal financial assistance." Similarly, Title II of the Americans with Disabilities Act provides that "no qualified individual with a disability shall, by reason of such disability, be excluded from participation in or be denied the benefits of the services, programs or activities of a public entity, or be subjected to discrimination by any such entity." Because of the great similarity in the requirements and scope of these provisions, courts frequently consider claims based on these laws together (see *K. M. v. Hyde Park Central School District*, 2005).

As noted earlier, courts considering these types of claims frequently analogize to *Davis*, reasoning that a school or district may be liable for student-on-student harassment based on the victim's disability when the school or district acted with deliberate indifference to harassment that was so severe, pervasive, and objectively offensive that it effectively denied the victim equal access to education resources and opportunities (see, e.g., *K. M. v. Hyde Park Central School District*, 2005). As with gender- and race-based harassment, the types of disability-based harassment activities (e.g., physical violence, name calling) that are adequate to meet this standard vary from court to court. There is at least some evidence, however, that, in contrast to other victims of peer harassment, mentally disabled victims may have a lower threshold to meet. Specifically, in some cases involving developmentally impaired victims, courts have expressed a greater willingness to find nonphysical acts, such verbal taunting or social isolation, adequately severe to meet the *Davis* standard (see, e.g., *K. M. v. Hyde Park Central School District*, 2005).

While the law clearly allows litigants to bring claims based on the Rehabilitation Act and the ADA against schools and districts receiving federal funds, the issue of individual liability under both of these provisions is currently unsettled. That is, although courts in some jurisdictions have determined that individuals, such as school teachers, principals, or other school employees, may be liable under the Rehabilitation Act and the ADA, courts in many other jurisdictions have not allowed litigants to bring such claims against individual defendants (see *Doe v. Town of Bourne*, 2004).

Claims against Individual School Employees

Section 1983 of the Civil Rights Act is a federal statute authorizing citizens to bring lawsuits to collect damages against state officials, such as schoolteachers, administrators, and other district employees, who have deprived them of their rights under federal law. In contrast to the previously discussed statutes, Section 1983 is specifically designed to allow lawsuits against individuals; these types of claims may not be brought against schools or districts as a whole. Claims based on this federal statute are commonly referred to simply as Section 1983 claims. The federal rights involved vary; in litigation related to incidents of bullying, the federal right in question is often the Fourteenth Amendment of the U.S. Constitution.

Two clauses of the Fourteenth Amendment are significant in this regard. First, the due process clause of the Fourteenth Amendment states that "no State shall . . . deprive any person of life, liberty, or property, without due process of law." Due process itself is often viewed as having two components: substantive due process and procedural due process. The former is the component typically implicated in lawsuits based on bullying incidents. Substantive due process provides individuals with protection against state legislation and other government action that infringes on protected rights and is violated when state officials engage in conduct of such an egregious nature as to shock one's conscience (*County of Sacramento v. Lewis*, 1998). This is a high standard to meet; negligently inflicted harm can never violate substantive due process (*County of Sacramento v. Lewis*, 1998). In fact, courts are generally reluctant to rely on substantive due process to impose liability on state officials for failing to prevent a person, such as a schoolchild, from being injured by a third party, such as another schoolchild (see *DeShaney v. Winnebago County Department of Social Services*, 1989). It is worth noting that there are two situations in which courts are more willing to find state officials liable for failing to prevent a person from injury from a third party (1) in cases involving persons in state custody and (2) in cases involving a state-created danger. For the most part, courts have found, however, that neither of these special circumstances exists in the typical school context. In the school violence context, some courts have gone even further to require deliberate indifference on the part of school officials in order to find liability for peer-on-peer harassment or attacks (see *Stevenson v. Martin County Board of Education*, 2001).

The second clause of the Fourteenth Amendment that is sometimes implicated in lawsuits related to incidents of bullying is the equal protection clause. The equal protection clause states that "no state shall . . . deny to any person within its jurisdiction the equal protection of the laws." To maintain an equal protection claim under Section 1983 of the Civil Rights Act, litigants must show that "the defendants, acting under color of state law, discriminated against them as members of an identifiable class and that the discrimination was intentional" (*Flores v. Morgan Hill Unified School District*, 2003). The discrimination may be based on any number of identifiable class characteristics, including, among others, gender, race, religion, sexual orientation, and disability. To show discrimination, plaintiffs essentially must provide evidence that the defendant school officials treated the plaintiffs differently than similarly situated individuals, such as by failing to enforce a school anti-harassment policy to prevent students from harassing gay students even though the officials enforced the policy to protect the rest of the student body.

Overall, there are numerous high hurdles for litigants bringing lawsuits in federal court for injuries arising out of school bullying incidents. Nonetheless, some litigants do succeed, particularly when the victim has suffered severe damages and school officials knew of a pattern of bullying by the perpetrator against the victim and yet did little or nothing to punish the perpetrator or prevent future incidents. For many victims of bullying, however, remedies under federal law are simply not available because the victim is not a member of a protected class as required under federal harassment law. These victims, therefore, may choose to bring suit under state law, as discussed further in the next section.

CLAIMS UNDER STATE LAW

In contrast to federal cases, state law cases related to incidents of school bullying are based on a much broader array of state laws, including privacy law, negligence, intentional inflic-tion of emotional distress, state discrimination law, and various provisions of state educa-tion codes, among others. The scope and enforceability of these laws vary greatly by state, depending on the exact wording of the statutes and state courts' interpretation of those statutes. Although remedies under state law generally may not be as attractive to litigants as those under federal law, bringing a claim under state law may be the only option for victims of bullying who are not members of a protected class and thus are not protected by federal harassment law. This gap in federal law is particularly noteworthy in light of research finding that victims of bullying are often bullied not because they possess any particular characteristic, such as race, gender, or disability, but simply because they are there.

One way in which state legislatures may be helping to plug this gap is through state anti-bullying legislation. The recent trend toward state anti-bullying legislation, dis-cussed in detail in the preceding sections, naturally raises the question as to whether liti-gants may bring legal claims against schools or officials failing to comply with these laws. Presently, this question remains largely unanswered. At least one court, however, has con-sidered this question. In the case of *Washington v. Pierce* (2005), the Vermont Supreme Court reviewed a student's claim that her school violated the provision of Vermont's bul-lying statute, which requires schools to create anti-bullying policies. Although the court determined there was insufficient evidence that the school's policy failed to meet the stat-ute's requirements, the fact that the court considered the claim at all suggests a willing-ness to allow claims based on the state's bullying law. Whether other states will follow suit remains to be seen.

CONCLUSIONS AND RECOMMENDATIONS

With recent heightened concerns about bullying and the many harms it may cause, it is incumbent on local educators to learn as much as possible about bullying and effective prevention and intervention approaches (see Chapters 2, 3, 6, and 7). In so doing, they should become intimately familiar with their state laws regarding bullying and any state-level model/sample policies that may exist. Whether or not they are required by state law, we encourage local boards of education (or other relevant policymakers) to develop policies on bullying for all grade levels. These local policies should be consistent with state laws and policies and informed by current research, which finds that bullying is best addressed through comprehensive schoolwide efforts implemented annually (Vreeman & Carroll, 2007). They should be developed through a process that involves input from all relevant stakeholders, including educators, parents, and students, and they should incorporate provisions for ongoing evaluation of all bullying prevention efforts in a school district. We do not recommend that any model policies be adopted verbatim. Although such policies may provide useful guidance to policymakers, local policies will be most effective where they reflect the unique assets and needs of the community. Developing and enforcing sound policies regarding bullying that focus on prevention will not only decrease the chances that legal action will be brought against schools and school districts, but, most importantly, it will also decrease the likelihood that children will suffer as the result of being bullied at school.

CASE EXAMPLE: THE CASE OF JESSII, AS TOLD BY HER MOTHER, JERI HAFFER

Jessii's father, whom Jessii adored, is a brilliant scientist and an introvert. Her mother is extroverted, owns and runs a gift shop, and in her spare time trains horses and saves the world. As a young child, Jessii was often called the Energizer bunny, a definite extrovert, a lover of life, an old soul, fascinated by people, and very perceptive. Jessii at a very early age wrote, "A soul cannot die."

Every morning Jessii's parents would take her to school and usually her mother would pick her up after school. Jessii had a bounce to her walk, as if the excitement of life filled her body and this excitement filled her body. Her mother looked forward to picking her up from school for she always has so many exciting things to share. She never missed a thing and seemed to bubble as she would talk about her day.

One day, in elementary school, while waiting for Jessii, her mother noticed that Jessii, who always held her head so high, looking up and around at everything, had her head down and her bounce was gone. Slowly she walked toward her mother looking at the ground. Jessii slid into the front seat and her mother asked, "What's wrong, Jessii?" Her mother was very worried, since this was not the happy, light-hearted daughter she knew. Jessii replied, "The teacher said we were worthless. She said I was no good and no one wanted me. She said she hated our family and we made her life living hell." Jessii's eyes began filling up with tears. "Do teachers lie to you, Mommy? They tell you if you see something bad happening to go tell the teacher. What do you do if they yell at you and say you are a trouble-maker and that no one likes you? They say you are a tattletale and everyone laughs at you." As Jessii's mother listened to her child, she became so upset that as soon as they got home she called a friend to take care of Jessii, and she went back to the school to confront Jessii's teacher.

The mother walked into the classroom that afternoon to find Jessii's teacher poring over some paperwork and clearly surprised to see her. Jessii's mother asked her if she had said those things to Jessii. The teacher looked shocked and said that Jessii was a great student. She didn't deny saying those words, but she said that she didn't say those things to Jessii. She shared that an incident had happened on the playground, but it didn't involve Jessii or her class. The mother then reasoned that Jessii was sensitive and internalized the playground incident that she observed. The teacher proceeded to tell Jessii's mother what a joy and a help Jessii was. She stated that Jessii was more mature than any student she had taught. Jessii's mother left feeling proud of her daughter.

What happened next did involve Jessii, and to this day her mother feels that this is more painful than she can express. Her mother feels that if she had not made the fateful promise, if they had moved, perhaps Jessii would not have taken her life. On another day in elementary school, her mother picked Jessii up from a friend's house and she was happy. She mentioned that she wanted to take some flowers to the nursing home to visit the elderly residents. Her mother said that they could do that on Saturday. Jessii called the residents at the nearby nursing home to arrange the visit. That night, Jessii and her mother read books as usual that evening after supper, and the next morning Jessii was her normal, happy self, and excited about going to school.

After school Jessii's mother waited for her and looked forward to her animated account of the day, only again to see her child's head hung down as she ran to the car. "Jessii, what's wrong?" The mother sensed alarm in her voice. "I can't tell you, Mom," she said as a tear rolled down her beautiful freckled cheek. "What do you mean you can't tell me?," her mother demanded. "Please, Mom, please! It will make it worse if I tell you." Now the tears that filled her beautiful brown eyes could not be contained and splashed on her cheeks. Her mother pleaded with her to tell her what was wrong. Then her mother said that she was going to talk to her teacher and Jessii screamed, begging her not to. Finally, still parked in front of the school, both in tears, Jessii said, "I can tell you if you promise." "What?" her mother asked. "Promise what? Why?" Jessii said, "Mom, remember you never make a promise unless you will keep it?" "Yes," her mother replied. Then Jessii said, "Mom, if you promise not to go to my teacher anymore, if you promise not to tell anyone, not even Daddy, then I can tell you. If you don't promise, there is no one I can tell." Her mother promised and now spends the rest of her life wishing she had never made that promise. She blames herself for her child's suicide. If only she had not promised.

That morning after Jessii went to her class, she was used as an example to teach the students not to tell their parents what happened in that teacher's classroom. Jessii was used as an example of a "baby" who had to "tattle to her mommy." All the children laughed at her and learned what would be in store for them if they told their parents about the verbal bullying that happened in the classroom. Jessii told her mother, "They all laughed at me, and then at recess they all punched me." Her mother saw her swollen arm and wanted to go to school to confront the teacher. Jessii pleaded and cried and said she had promised not to go to school. She begged her mother not to make it worse. Her parents wanted to remove her from the school. They even talked to the superintendent. Sadly, Jessii was right; the bullying did get worse. Jessii was bullied for a variety of reasons: She was the only Jewish student in the school; she was smart; her family was seen as wealthy; she defended other students who were being picked on; and the community was wary of "outsiders." Despite the constant bullying, Jessii said she didn't want to leave her school. Her mother remembers her begging her not to tell her father about the continued bullying and her mother agreed. She didn't tell her husband and she didn't go back to the school. The bullying got worse and continued throughout elementary school and into junior high school. Jessii's mother promised not to tell and, although Jessii was a third-degree black belt, she never defended herself.

"What do you want?" That was the question the school superintendent asked Jessii's parents after she committed suicide when she was 14 years old. The principals and counselors from the elementary and high schools were at the meeting. "All we really want is our daughter back!" Jessii's parents wanted to scream. However, they didn't say this. Jessii's parents were not sure about miracles of that magnitude so they asked for a small thing that the administrators actually were able to deliver. Jessii's parents asked for change.

They were all afraid of a lawsuit, and Jessii's parents had been told that they could have sued and won. Everyone knew it. There were enough witnesses, enough of a paper trail, and Jessii's parents had gotten a court order to look at some computers for even more evidence. However, they felt that none of that retribution would have brought their child back and, most importantly, they felt that Jessii wouldn't have wanted that. They felt that their child was a child of forgiveness and unconditional love. She was never a child of condemnation, never a bitter child.

Thoughts about Jessii's Case

"Change is what we want," Jessii's parents said. They wanted the school and all schools to be safe places where children wanted to go to learn. Jessii always wanted to go to school and she was an extrovert who loved people and loved to learn about everything. Jessii didn't like the lies and gossip encouraged by and sometimes started by teachers. She didn't like the labels put on students by teachers or the ignorance, injustice, the blatant favoritism that was often religious and socioeconomically based. The small town in which Jessii lived was, in many ways, an example of inclusion and exclusion, often based on sports, religious beliefs, and who was related to whom. Given some of these small-town exclusionary criteria, Jessii was completely ostracized. Her family wasn't "from here," and many people in this small town could not understand why a Jewish family moved to this rural community and now, after their daughter is gone, why do they stay? However, they stay for the hope that change can happen and for the connection that they have to Jessii, to the community where she lived and for which she gave her life.

FOLLOW-UP QUESTIONS

1. For more details about Jessii's experience, you can read an article in the *Omaha World-Herald* at *www.advantagebio.com/Stories.htm*. What are some of the details that stand out to you? How can Jessii's story be used to affect change?

2. Jessii's parents decided not to sue the school district because they felt that a lawsuit wouldn't bring about change. How does change happen? In this case, do you think that a lawsuit would have changed how people treat each other?

3. A similar theme that we hear over and over again is that in many small towns there is intolerance toward differences. How can our families and schools work to embrace all children and families regardless of religious orientation, sexual orientation, gender, and other characteristics? What do you do to teach tolerance?

4. Think about the most compelling point(s) of Jessii and her parents' story. How can you carry forth her legacy so more lives are not lost as a result of bullying?

6

Using Your Own Resources to Combat Bullying

One of our colleagues tells a story about going to a school and the vice principal told him, "We love your anti-bullying program!" Our colleague said, "That's great. How is it working?" The vice principal replied, "I don't know. It's still in the box in my office!" This story reminds us that effective bullying prevention and intervention really are not about buying a specific program. They are about changing social relationships so that they are healthy, not dysfunctional. Our premise is that if we model and help students develop healthy social relationships, then, by definition, bullying behaviors cannot occur. In addition to asking the question "What are the conditions that allow bullying/victimization behaviors to occur?," we believe that "it's the people who matter, not the program." People create healthy social relationships, and the adults in our schools should teach students how to be respectful, kind, and helpful toward one another.

The focus of this chapter is to help school personnel analyze the social climate among staff and students and to figure out ways to use the data gathered to enhance social relationships. Following the introduction of our data-based decision-making model, we focus on assessing the social climate, strengthening home–school connections, strengthening school–community connections, and improving the quality of social relationships in order to prevent and reduce bullying behaviors. We provide an example of how an elementary school infused bullying awareness and prevention into a third-grade literature unit called the "Bullying Literature Project." There are many creative ways in which schools and staff can address bullying prevention and intervention without having to buy expensive programs or hire expensive consultants. We too often hear, "We can't afford program X or program Y; therefore, we don't know what to do about the bullying." Our response is to assert that modeling and fostering healthy social relationships and creating conditions where bullying behaviors cannot occur is free!

DATA-BASED DECISION MAKING

We have previously written about a data-based decision-making rubric for guiding bullying prevention and intervention programming (Figure 6.1; Swearer & Espelage, 2004). The time has come for a data-based approach to bullying prevention and intervention in our schools. The finding that less than a fourth of more than 300 violence prevention and school-based programs on the market are empirically validated (Howard, Flora, & Griffin, 1999) indicates we are not doing so well. The time has long passed for parents, educators, and researchers to collect and use their own data to make decisions about bullying prevention and intervention efforts. We hope this chapter helps parents, educators, and researchers think about how to use data to inform practice and to ultimately reduce or eradicate bullying in their schools and communities.

The rubric in Figure 6.1 is a guide to help school personnel think about ways to collect data on bullying/victimization and then use these data to make decisions. One example that we often share is about a middle school where the staff collected data every spring. The school administration, staff, parents, and students had all made a commitment to collect data each spring and used these data to make decisions about bullying prevention and intervention (described in more detail in Chapter 9). One year the students reported that bullying occurred in the hallway 30% of the time, and then the following year this percentage had increased to 70%. What accounted for the significant increase in bullying between

1. Partner with university researchers to conduct an assessment of bullying behaviors.

2. Conduct a schoolwide, *anonymous* assessment of bullying behaviors.

3. Use multiple informants in any assessment to obtain different perspectives (students, teachers, school staff, parents).

4. Use self-report, peer report, teacher report, and observations, if possible.

5. Graph data to create a picture of the scope of the bullying behaviors in a particular school or classroom.

6. Use the data to conduct classroom presentations on bullying.

7. Use the data to create interventions for bullying.

8. Use the data to establish preventive measures to create an anti-bullying climate.

9. Share the data with parent groups (e.g., parent–teacher organization).

10. Create a data-based decision-making climate through the use of individual school and/or classroom data to help guide prevention and intervention strategies.

FIGURE 6.1. Rubric for data-based decision making in bullying prevention and intervention strategies. Adapted from Swearer and Espelage (2004). Copyright 2004 by Lawrence Erlbaum Associates. Adapted by permission of Taylor and Francis Group, LLC, a division of Informa plc.

these 2 years? What happened was that the school administration had added 1 minute of time between classes from year 1 to year 2. After looking at the data, the school administration decided to "take back" the extra minute of time between classes, and the following year the bullying in the hallways was reduced. Quite simply, with the extra minute, the students had too much time on their hands, and they were able to engage in bullying in the hallways. When the minute was taken away, the condition (i.e., too much time) that allowed the bullying to occur was eliminated. This is an excellent example of data-based decision making and a free intervention. We are strong advocates of schools and communities using existing resources to alter the conditions under which bullying can occur. Next, we outline the specific components of developing a data-based decision-making climate that everyone, in every community and in every school, can do.

STEP 1: GATHER DATA

Anyone can collect data! First, we recommend conducting a comprehensive survey assessment of bullying behaviors in your school. There are many bullying surveys on the market, and their description is beyond the scope of this book. However, each school and community typically has unique characteristics that not all surveys might capture. Create an anti-bullying committee (if your school does not already have one), have the committee collect sample surveys, and then choose the survey that best fits your school's climate and needs.

The development of an anti-bullying committee composed of administration, teachers, parents, and students is *vital*. Establishing this committee communicates that the commitment to anti-bullying initiatives is a priority of your school and community. Sadly, we see in some schools and communities that the people who are trying to do something about bullying are seen as "oversensitive" and focusing on a problem that "isn't there." We firmly believe that the support of principals, school boards, and Departments of Education on behalf of anti-bullying initiatives is a critical component for effectively reducing bullying behaviors.

Assessment of School Climate (or Social Climate)

The elements that comprise the concept of "school climate" have been widely studied (Kasen et al., 2004). The factors that contribute to a healthy school climate are vital to preventing bullying problems in schools. We know that positive school climate is vital for safe and healthy schools (Sprague & Walker, 2005). Not only are there school climate surveys that can be used to assess school climate, but there are also commonsense practices that either facilitate or undermine healthy school climate. Consider the following example: At one middle school, as part of a school spirit activity, the students and staff advertise "identical day." On identical day, the students decide to dress like their friends. While on the surface this seems like a fun idea, it actually sets the stage for relational aggression. What if only the cool kids wear a certain shirt on identical day? What if one student says to another that he or she will dress identically and then they don't? Schools can inadvertently set the conditions that will encourage bullying behaviors. As much as possible, the adults in the school setting should examine policies and practices to see whether these activities actually set the stage for bullying behaviors.

We also believe that it is critical to collect data anonymously. We are often asked whether or not it is good practice to list the names of all the students in the school and then have their peers identify them as "bullies" or "victims." This, quite simply, is *not* good practice. Having students identify by name bullies and victims serves to further support the myth that bullying/victimization is a problem that is dyadic in nature when we know that it is not (Espelage & Swearer, 2003). This type of identification also perpetuates the notion of blaming the bully and shaming the victim. Additionally, this type of investigation actually poisons the school climate by encouraging students to focus on negative attributes in their peers and maybe even to set up peers by falsely accusing them. On the other hand, anonymous surveys that query students about the locations where bullying takes place, the types of bullying students experience, and other details about the behaviors serve to increase awareness about the nature of bullying in a particular school. Armed with this information, school personnel and students can work together to create the conditions to reduce bullying (see Chapter 9 for an example).

STEP 2: INCREASE AWARENESS ABOUT BULLYING BEHAVIORS

With the increase in attention given to bullying in the research literature, there has also been a parallel increase in children's literature on bullying. In terms of student-friendly ways to increase awareness regarding the consequences of bullying, this is a great opportunity for libraries and media centers to order books that address bullying. Using literature to increase awareness of a problem and to help solve problems is called *bibliotherapy*. It has been suggested that bibliotherapy is an excellent tool for working with students who are experiencing bullying/victimization problems (Gregory & Vessey, 2004).

In an effort to evaluate potential bibliotherapy books for dealing with bullying/victimization, we worked with a third-grade team of students and teachers. We were interested in elementary school student and teacher ratings of different children's books about bullying (i.e., the Bullying Literature Project). In this project, we worked with a group of six third-grade teachers and 102 third-grade students. The third grade at Maxey Elementary School

(text continues on page 85)

TABLE 6.1. Selected Elementary School Books about Bullying

1. Trudy Ludwig, *My Secret Bully* (2005). Berkeley, CA: Tricycle Press.
2. Madonna, *The English Roses* (2003). New York: Callaway Editions.
3. Phil Roxbee Cox, *Don't Be a Bully, Billy: A Cautionary Tale* (2004). London: Usborne.
4. Catherine DePino, *Blue Cheese Breath and Stinky Feet: How to Deal with Bullies* (2004). Washington, DC: Magination Press.
5. Joanna Cole, *Bully Trouble* (1989). New York: Random House.
6. Shabana Mir, *Umar and the Bully* (2007). Leicestershire, UK: Islamic Foundation.
7. Stan and Jan Berenstain, *The Berenstain Bears and the Bully* (1993). New York: Random House.
8. Trevor Romain, *Bullies Are a Pain in the Brain* (1997). Minneapolis, MN: Free Spirit.
9. Marissa Moss, *Amelia's Bully Survival Guide* (2006). New York: Simon & Schuster.
10. Alexis O'Neill and Laura Huliska-Beith, *The Recess Queen* (2002). New York: Scholastic Press.
11. Trevor Romain, *Cliques, Phonies, and Other Baloney* (1998). Minneapolis, MN: Free Spirit.
12. Kate Cohen-Posey, *How to Handle Bullies, Teasers and Other Meanies: A Book That Takes the Nuisance Out of Name Calling and Other Nonsense* (1995). Highland City, FL: Rainbow Books.
13. Cari Best, *Shrinking Violet* (2001). New York: Farrar, Straus & Giroux.
14. Derek Munson, *Enemy Pie* (2000). San Francisco: Chronicle Books.
15. Patty Lovell, *Stand Tall, Molly Lou Melon* (2001). New York: Putnam.
16. Peggy Moss, *Say Something* (2004). Gardiner, ME: Tilbury House.
17. Gershen Kaufman, Lev Raphael, and Pamela Espeland, *Stick Up for Yourself!: Every Kid's Guide to Personal Power and Positive Self-Esteem* (1999). Minneapolis, MN: Free Spirit.
18. Nancy Carlson, *How to Lose All Your Friends* (1997). New York: Puffin.
19. Dana Smith-Mansell, *Stop Bullying Bobby!: Helping Children Cope with Teasing and Bullying* (2004). Far Hills, NJ: New Horizon Press.
20. Phyllis Reynolds Naylor, *King of the Playground* (1994). New York: Aladdin.
21. Pat Thomas, *Stop Picking on Me: A First Look at Bullying* (2000). Hauppauge, NY: Barron's Educational Series.
22. Karen Gedig Burnett, *Simon's Hook: A Story about Teases and Put-Downs* (1999). Felton, CA: GR Publishing.
23. Steve Siskin and Allen Shamblin, *Don't Laugh at Me* (2002). Berkeley, CA: Tricycle Press.
24. Becky Ray McCain, *Nobody Knew What to Do: A Story about Bullying* (2001). Morton Grove, IL: Albert Whitman.

TABLE 6.2. Mean Ratings for Bullying Literature Project for Teachers

Book title	Number of raters	Mean[a]
My Secret Bully	3	
Taught about bullying		1.33
What to *do* about bullying		1.67
Use book in teaching		1.33
Easy to understand		1.33
Overall rating		1.33
The English Roses	6	
Taught about bullying		1.67
What to *do* about bullying		1.67
Use book in teaching		2.00
Easy to understand		1.67
Overall rating		1.67
Don't Be a Bully, Billy: A Cautionary Tale	4	
Taught about bullying		2.50
What to *do* about bullying		3.00
Use book in teaching		3.00
Easy to understand		2.00
Overall rating		2.75
Blue Cheese Breath and Stinky Feet: How to Deal with Bullies	5	
Taught about bullying		1.20
What to *do* about bullying		1.40
Use book in teaching		1.40
Easy to understand		1.40
Overall rating		1.40
Bully Trouble	3	
Taught about bullying		1.33
What to *do* about bullying		2.00
Use book in teaching		2.33
Easy to understand		1.67
Overall rating		2.33
Umar and the Bully	4	
Taught about bullying		1.30
What to *do* about bullying		1.50
Use book in teaching		2.50
Easy to understand		2.30
Overall rating		2.00
The Berenstain Bears and the Bully	5	
Taught about bullying		1.80
What to *do* about bullying		2.00
Use book in teaching		2.40
Easy to understand		1.60
Overall rating		2.00

(continued)

TABLE 6.2. (continued)

Book title	Number of raters	Mean[a]
Bullies Are a Pain in the Brain	3	
Taught about bullying		1.00
What to *do* about bullying		1.00
Use book in teaching		1.30
Easy to understand		1.66
Overall rating		1.66
Amelia's Bully Survival Guide	4	
Taught about bullying		2.00
What to *do* about bullying		2.00
Use book in teaching		3.00
Easy to understand		2.25
Overall rating		2.25
The Recess Queen	6	
Taught about bullying		1.60
What to *do* about bullying		1.83
Use book in teaching		1.67
Easy to understand		1.50
Overall rating		1.50
Cliques, Phonies, and Other Baloney	3	
Taught about bullying		1.66
What to *do* about bullying		1.66
Use book in teaching		2.00
Easy to understand		1.66
Overall rating		1.66
How to Handle Bullies, Teasers and Other Meanies: A Book That Takes the Nuisance Out of Name Calling and Other Nonsense	3	
Taught about bullying		1.00
What to *do* about bullying		1.00
Use book in teaching		1.00
Easy to understand		1.00
Overall rating		1.00
Shrinking Violet	6	
Taught about bullying		2.00
What to *do* about bullying		2.33
Use book in teaching		2.33
Easy to understand		2.33
Overall rating		2.00
Enemy Pie	5	
Taught about bullying		1.80
What to *do* about bullying		1.60
Use book in teaching		1.40
Easy to understand		1.20
Overall rating		1.50

(continued)

TABLE 6.2. (*continued*)

Book title	Number of raters	Mean[a]
Stand Tall, Molly Lou Melon	5	
Taught about bullying		2.00
What to *do* about bullying		2.20
Use book in teaching		2.20
Easy to understand		1.80
Overall rating		2.00
Say Something	5	
Taught about bullying		1.40
What to *do* about bullying		1.20
Use book in teaching		1.40
Easy to understand		1.40
Overall rating		1.40
Stick Up for Yourself!: Every Kid's Guide to Personal Power and Positive Self-Esteem	2	
Taught about bullying		2.00
What to *do* about bullying		1.50
Use book in teaching		2.00
Easy to understand		2.00
Overall rating		2.00
How to Lose All Your Friends	4	
Taught about bullying		2.50
What to *do* about bullying		3.50
Use book in teaching		3.00
Easy to understand		2.00
Overall rating		2.75
Stop Bullying Bobby!: Helping Children Cope with Teasing and Bullying	2	
Taught about bullying		1.50
What to *do* about bullying		1.50
Use book in teaching		1.50
Easy to understand		1.50
Overall rating		1.50
King of the Playground	5	
Taught about bullying		2.00
What to *do* about bullying		2.00
Use book in teaching		3.00
Easy to understand		3.00
Overall rating		3.00
Stop Picking on Me: A First Look at Bullying	5	
Taught about bullying		1.60
What to *do* about bullying		1.80
Use book in teaching		2.40
Easy to understand		1.75
Overall rating		2.00

(*continued*)

TABLE 6.2. *(continued)*

Book title	Number of raters	Mean[a]
Simon's Hook: A Story about Teases and Put-Downs	5	
Taught about bullying		1.60
What to *do* about bullying		1.40
Use book in teaching		1.60
Easy to understand		1.80
Overall rating		1.60
Don't Laugh at Me	5	
Taught about bullying		1.80
What to *do* about bullying		2.60
Use book in teaching		2.60
Easy to understand		1.80
Overall rating		2.00
Nobody Knew What to Do: A Story about Bullying	4	
Taught about bullying		1.75
What to *do* about bullying		1.25
Use book in teaching		1.75
Easy to understand		1.00
Overall rating		1.50

[a]Lower numbers are better: 1 = *strongly agree*; 2 = *agree*; 3 = *disagree*; 4 = *strongly disagree*.

TABLE 6.3. Mean Ratings for Bullying Literature Project for Students

Book title	Number of raters	Mean[a]
My Secret Bully	96	
Taught about bullying		1.76
What to *do* about bullying		1.84
Recommend to a friend		1.96
Easy to understand		1.67
The English Roses	94	
Taught about bullying		2.03
What to *do* about bullying		2.18
Recommend to a friend		1.76
Easy to understand		1.51
Don't Be a Bully, Billy: A Cautionary Tale	96	
Taught about bullying		1.82
What to *do* about bullying		1.50
Recommend to a friend		1.94
Easy to understand		1.67

(continued)

TABLE 6.3. *(continued)*

Book title	Number of raters	Mean[a]
Blue Cheese Breath and Stinky Feet: How to Deal with Bullies	75	
Taught about bullying		1.53
What to *do* about bullying		1.53
Recommend to a friend		1.66
Easy to understand		1.69
Bully Trouble	98	
Taught about bullying		1.50
What to *do* about bullying		1.94
Recommend to a friend		1.67
Easy to understand		1.51
Umar and the Bully	71	
Taught about bullying		1.42
What to *do* about bullying		1.54
Recommend to a friend		1.77
Easy to understand		1.56
The Berenstain Bears and the Bully	74	
Taught about bullying		1.69
What to *do* about bullying		2.31
Recommend to a friend		1.74
Easy to understand		1.55
Bullies Are a Pain in the Brain	76	
Taught about bullying		1.46
What to *do* about bullying		1.43
Recommend to a friend		1.63
Easy to understand		1.41
Amelia's Bully Survival Guide	52	
Taught about bullying		1.88
What to *do* about bullying		2.15
Recommend to a friend		2.02
Easy to understand		1.77
The Recess Queen	94	
Taught about bullying		1.76
What to *do* about bullying		2.04
Recommend to a friend		1.61
Easy to understand		1.50
Cliques, Phonies, and Other Baloney	17	
Taught about bullying		1.76
What to *do* about bullying		1.88
Recommend to a friend		1.41
Easy to understand		1.53

(continued)

TABLE 6.3. *(continued)*

Book title	Number of raters	Mean[a]
How to Handle Bullies, Teasers and Other Meanies: A Book That Takes the Nuisance Out of Name Calling and Other Nonsense	20	
Taught about bullying		1.25
What to *do* about bullying		1.10
Recommend to a friend		2.05
Easy to understand		1.5
Shrinking Violet	97	
Taught about bullying		2.08
What to *do* about bullying		2.16
Recommend to a friend		1.92
Easy to understand		1.79
Enemy Pie	99	
Taught about bullying		2.23
What to *do* about bullying		1.92
Recommend to a friend		1.65
Easy to understand		1.46
Stand Tall, Molly Lou Melon	96	
Taught about bullying		2.23
What to *do* about bullying		2.21
Recommend to a friend		1.80
Easy to understand		1.74
Say Something	92	
Taught about bullying		1.91
What to *do* about bullying		2.23
Recommend to a friend		2.08
Easy to understand		1.75
Stick Up for Yourself!: Every Kid's Guide to Personal Power and Positive Self-Esteem	0	
Taught about bullying		
What to *do* about bullying		
Recommend to a friend		
Easy to understand		
How to Lose All Your Friends	73	
Taught about bullying		2.73
What to *do* about bullying		3.41
Recommend to a friend		2.41
Easy to understand		2.26
Stop Bullying Bobby!: Helping Children Cope with Teasing and Bullying	57	
Taught about bullying		1.79
What to *do* about bullying		1.88
Recommend to a friend		1.63
Easy to understand		1.89

(continued)

TABLE 6.3.　*(continued)*

Book title	Number of raters	Mean[a]
King of the Playground	97	
Taught about bullying		1.89
What to *do* about bullying		1.84
Recommend to a friend		1.91
Easy to understand		1.67
Stop Picking on Me: A First Look at Bullying	83	
Taught about bullying		1.67
What to *do* about bullying		2.02
Recommend to a friend		2.06
Easy to understand		1.58
Simon's Hook: A Story about Teases and Put-Downs	73	
Taught about bullying		1.70
What to *do* about bullying		1.79
Recommend to a friend		1.58
Easy to understand		1.52
Don't Laugh at Me	93	
Taught about bullying		2.11
What to *do* about bullying		2.57
Recommend to a friend		2.05
Easy to understand		1.76
Nobody Knew What to Do: A Story about Bullying	70	
Taught about bullying		1.99
What to *do* about bullying		1.76
Recommend to a friend		2.03
Easy to understand		1.57

[a]Lower numbers are better: 1 = *strongly agree*; 2 = *agree*; 3 = *disagree*; 4 = *strongly disagree*.

in Lincoln, Nebraska participated in the project in fall 2006. We chose books on bullying that were geared toward an elementary school audience (books are listed in Table 6.1). The students and their teachers read and rated these books, and their results are listed in Tables 6.2 and 6.3. The teacher and student rating forms are in Appendices 6.1 and 6.2 (at the end of the chapter) and can be reproduced for use. The purpose of the Bullying Literature Project was to increase awareness about the consequences of bullying and to teach the students how to critically evaluate what they were reading. The project became part of the reading curriculum, and the teachers were able to incorporate the project in their lesson planning. Because it was part of the reading curriculum, reading books about bullying was not seen as an additional burden. The Media Center specialist coordinated with the third-grade team and ordered many of the books listed in Table 6.1 for the media center. It is also feasible that the recording and analysis of the data could be part of the math curriculum and creating graphs from the data could be part of the technology curriculum. Thus, a project like this can span different curricula and can also serve to increase awareness about bullying.

Bullying Literature Project: Teacher and Student Data

Six third-grade teachers (five women and one man) participated in the Bullying Literature Project. They had taught for an average of 15.67 years, with a mean of 2.67 years teaching at Maxey Elementary School. They were all European American. The mean ratings for each of the 24 books are listed in Table 6.2. The teacher's top five highest rated books about bullying were (1) *How to Handle Bullies, Teasers and Other Meanies: A Book That Takes the Nuisance Out of Name Calling and Other Nonsense*; (2) *Bullies Are a Pain in the Brain*; (3) *Blue Cheese Breath and Stinky Feet: How to Deal with Bullies*; (4) *Say Something*; and (5) *My Secret Bully.*

One hundred two third graders, ages 8–9, participated in the Bullying Literature Project. Of these, 98% were native English speakers, 87% were European American, and 47% were girls and 54% were boys. Their mean ratings for each of the 24 books are listed in Table 6.3. The students' top five most-liked books in terms of teaching about bullying were (1) *How to Handle Bullies, Teasers and Other Meanies: A Book That Takes the Nuisance Out of Name Calling and Other Nonsense*; (2) *Bullies Are a Pain in the Brain*; (3) *Umar and the Bully*; (4) *Blue Cheese Breath and Stinky Feet: How to Deal with Bullies*; and (5) *Bully Trouble.*

It is interesting that three books received top ratings by both teachers and students. Thus, the students and teachers felt that these three books were the most helpful in terms of teaching about bullying behaviors. For elementary schools with limited resources, we suggest purchasing these three books. The students and teachers reported enjoying the Bullying Literature Project. It was a great way to introduce books about bullying that were developmentally appropriate, and because it was part of the third-grade literature unit, it was not an "add-on." The teachers incorporated critical thinking skills into the unit, and students enjoyed completing the rating forms on each book. The students wrote several comments about what they learned, including "I learned not to ever bully or nobody will play with you or want to be your friend," "If someone is being mean to you, just don't play with them," "If someone else looks like they're lonely, you should ask if they want to play," "It taught me that bullying hurts. Don't bully," "If someone is getting bullied, don't stand around," "If somebody is getting bullied, tell an adult and they will take care of it," and "Don't let bullies get your attention, because that is what they want from you."

STEP 3: ENHANCE HOME–SCHOOL RELATIONSHIPS

When we view bullying as a breakdown of our social relationships, the relationships that school and families forge become paramount in effective bullying prevention and intervention. If school personnel and families are in a negative relationship, children and adolescents observe the adults in their lives in conflict. Frequently, we hear stories about parents being angry with school personnel and feeling unsupported. More frequently, we hear sto-

ries about school personnel who feel that the student's parents or caregivers are not supportive of the school. When these conflicts between families and schools occur, students do not observe healthy adult relationships or healthy conflict resolution. Fostering long-term relationships between schools and families is an ongoing interaction that requires constant communication and nurturing of the relationship (Christenson & Sheridan, 2001). School personnel should constantly involve parents in the educational process through home–school communications (e.g., notes, e-mail), school activities, and classroom activities. Parents should continually think about how they can be supportive of their child's teacher and schools (e.g., attending parent–teacher conferences, volunteering in the classroom, helping with school activities). Creating a positive connection between families and schools helps create healthy relationships among students, parents, and schools. In turn, this sets the stage for fostering positive relationships and for eliminating the conditions that allow bullying behaviors to occur.

STEP 4: ENHANCE COMMUNITY–SCHOOL RELATIONSHIPS

Many schools across the United States have business or community partners who support programming, funding, and school activities. These types of community–school relationships are vital for schools. The TeamMates mentoring program in the State of Nebraska is an example of a positive community–school relationship. TeamMates was founded in 1991 by Dr. Tom Osborne and his wife, Nancy. TeamMates is a school-based mentoring program in which a community adult volunteer is paired with a student who needs additional support to maintain a positive trajectory to graduate from high school. In Lincoln, Nebraska, the program currently serves 550 students in grades 4 through 12. Successful school–community partnerships are collaborative and positive, focus on student achievement and success, and maintain a commitment to diversity (Sheridan, Napolitano, & Swearer, 2002). TeamMates is an excellent example of an important community–school connection. Currently, TeamMates has partnered with the Target Bullying Project at the University of Nebraska–Lincoln to evaluate the effectiveness of mentoring on bullying/victimization experiences among students in the program. We are predicting that healthy community–school relationships developed through the TeamMates program will reduce bullying behaviors and will help students who are victimized to feel supported and helped.

STEP 5: MAKE A COMMITMENT
TO CHANGE THE SOCIAL CLIMATE

Keeping in mind the 80/20 principle (Koch, 1998), we know that, unless the majority of the individuals in a community are supportive of a concept, idea, or a program, it will fail. Thus, collective implementation of any bullying prevention and intervention programming is the foundation for changing the conditions that allow bullying to occur (Orpinas & Horne, 2006). It really does take an "entire village" to change the social climate (Clinton, 1996) and to combat bullying behaviors effectively.

CONCLUSIONS AND RECOMMENDATIONS

It is not complicated for school personnel to use their own resources to combat bullying/victimization. In order to develop healthy social relationships, adults first need to model healthy social relationships. Figure 6.2 illustrates steps that should be followed to engage in healthy communication. School districts and school personnel need to develop a system for gathering data to assess the scope of bullying/victimization in their schools. Increasing awareness about bullying behaviors is vital. What does your school and/or community do to increase this awareness? Infusing bullying awareness across the curricula is a great first step. Working directly and openly with parents and community leaders has great potential for helping reduce bullying behaviors among our nation's youth.

CASE EXAMPLE: BEN—THE MYSTERY OF THE ACHING BACK

Ben's parents were perplexed as to why his back was hurting so much. He would come home from school with a backache on most days. Ben was short for his age and generally small in stature but had always been physically fit and healthy. He was complaining so much that his parents finally took him to his doctor to see if something could be done to alleviate his pain. Ben's doctor recommended a physical therapist to work with Ben on some exercises to strengthen his back and improve his posture. In the initial meeting with the physical therapist, she did a comprehensive intake with Ben and his parents. During the interview, she asked if Ben was carrying his backpack on one shoulder or two. Ben said that he normally carried his backpack on one shoulder, and the physical therapist commented that this can cause a lot of back pain for some students. Ben's parents quickly interjected that Ben only carries his backpack from where they drop him off to his locker. This could hardly cause him any back pain. However, Ben shared that he actually was carrying his backpack with him all day. Additionally, he had been keeping all of his textbooks and materials in his backpack at all times.

Ben's parents were surprised at this news because their son had many heavy textbooks and school materials. When asked why he was doing this, Ben became uncomfortable and tried to avoid the discussion. When pressed to provide an answer, he stated that his locker

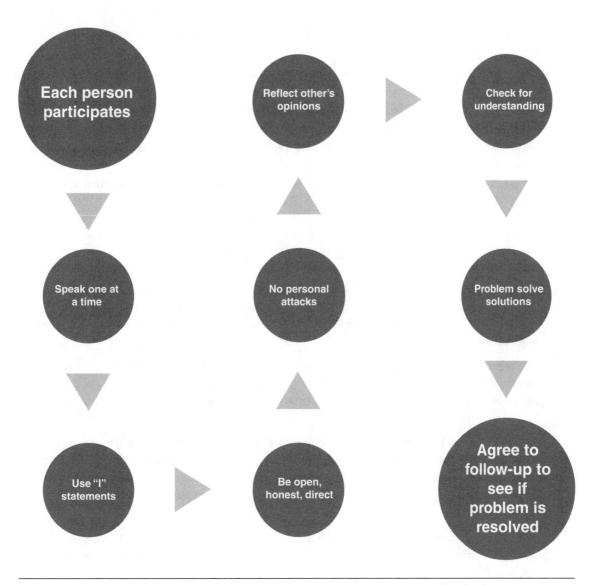

FIGURE 6.2. Ground rules for respectful communication between parents and school personnel.

partner was teasing and bullying him so much that he began to avoid using his locker. In fact, he hadn't been to his locker in over a month.

Ben's parents were initially very upset with Ben for not sharing this information sooner. He told them that he had been trying to handle the situation on his own and did not want to involve his parents or teachers for fear that the teasing would increase. Once Ben talked with his parents, they all went to talk to the school principal together. The principal was very open to moving Ben to a new locker area. Since he has been using his locker, his back pain has disappeared.

FOLLOW-UP QUESTIONS

1. In this case, the simple solution was to have Ben move his locker. The school administration was supportive of Ben and his parents, and they all worked together to solve the bullying problem by simply having Ben move lockers. Think of some examples in your school where a simple solution solved a bullying problem.

2. The principal was supportive and open to the idea of this student switching his locker. Are all school administrators so supportive? Do all parents create conditions where their children will talk openly about their problems? While the answer is "No," what can you do to create healthy home–school relationships?

3. Students who are being bullied typically do not talk to adults (teachers or parents) about their experiences for fear it will get worse or concern that adults can't help. What supports are in place at your school where students can talk about their experiences? Are there school counselors, school psychologists, social workers, mentors, or other additional support personnel who are there for students?

4. What type of school–community connections does your school have? How might fostering school–community connections create conditions that will foster healthy, positive relationships?

Bullying Literature Project—Teacher Evaluation Form

Your name: _____

Name of school: _____

Are you female or male? (circle one)   Female   Male

Years teaching: _____

Years teaching at this school: _____

Race:

___ White/European American

___ Asian American

___ Black/African American

___ Native American

___ Latino(a)/Hispanic

___ Middle Eastern

___ Eastern European

___ Asian

___ Biracial (Please specify: _____)

___ Other (Please specify: _____)

Bullying is a problem among the students in our school.

Strongly Agree	Agree	Disagree	Strongly Disagree
O	O	O	O

Bullying is a problem among the staff in our school.

Strongly Agree	Agree	Disagree	Strongly Disagree
O	O	O	O

(continued)

Title of the book: _____

Author: _____ Today's date: __/__/__

1.   This book taught my students about bullying. (Please fill in one circle below.)

Strongly	Agree	Disagree	Strongly
Agree			Disagree
O	O	O	O

2.   This book taught my students WHAT TO DO about bullying. (Please fill in one circle below.)

Strongly	Agree	Disagree	Strongly
Agree			Disagree
O	O	O	O

3.   I would use this book in my teaching. (Please fill in one circle below.)

Strongly	Agree	Disagree	Strongly
Agree			Disagree
O	O	O	O

4.   The author made the information easy to understand. (Please fill in one circle below.)

Strongly	Agree	Disagree	Strongly
Agree			Disagree
O	O	O	O

5.   My overall rating of the book is: (Please fill in one circle below.)

| Excellent | Average | Poor | Awful |
| O | O | O | O |

THANK YOU

Bullying Literature Project—Student Evaluation Form

Your name: _____

Are you a girl or boy? (circle one)   Girl   Boy

How old are you?   _____ years

Is English the first language you learned to speak? __ Yes   __ No

How well do you do in your schoolwork? On your last report card, if you think about all of your subjects, what did you get? (Check one.)

_____ Mostly 4s   _____ 4s and 3s   _____ Mostly 3s

_____ 3s and 2s   _____ Mostly 2s   _____ 2s and lower

Race:

__ White/European American

__ Asian American

__ Black/African American

__ Native American

__ Latino(a)/Hispanic

__ Middle Eastern

__ Eastern European

__ Asian

__ Biracial (Please specify: ___)

__ Other (Please specify: ____)

(continued)

Title of the book: _____

Author: _____ Today's date: __/__/__

1. This book taught me about bullying. (Please fill in one circle below.)

Strongly Agree	Agree	Disagree	Strongly Disagree
O	O	O	O

2. This book taught me WHAT TO DO about bullying. (Please fill in one circle below.)

Strongly Agree	Agree	Disagree	Strongly Disagree
O	O	O	O

3. I would recommend this book to a friend. (Please fill in one circle below.)

Strongly Agree	Agree	Disagree	Strongly Disagree
O	O	O	O

4. This book made sense to me. (Please fill in one circle below.)

Strongly Agree	Agree	Disagree	Strongly Disagree
O	O	O	O

5. Please write down anything else you learned from reading this book.

7

Practical Strategies
to Reduce Bullying

In order to reduce bullying behaviors among school-age youth, interventions targeting the social ecology are vital. If we view bullying as a social relationship problem (Chapter 3), then it stands to reason that improving social functioning is a key element in reducing bullying behaviors. In this chapter, we discuss practical strategies across the individual, peer, family, school, community, and societal domains that can improve social functioning and, in turn, reduce bullying. It is our assertion that, to effectively reduce bullying, coordinated interventions across the social ecology are vital (see Chapter 2). Remembering the 80/20 principle, targeted interventions will have the greatest impact and will create lasting, meaningful change.

WHAT ABOUT PUNISHMENT?

We live in a society where punishment-based strategies are often the first line of defense against students' behavioral problems. A student bullies someone else, and we want to see that "bully" punished for his or her behaviors. However, recent research is suggesting that punishment-based strategies may not be the most effective strategy (Skiba et al., 2006). We also want to note that punishment-based strategies (i.e., zero tolerance, expulsion, suspension) for youth who bully others are typically not effective (Casella, 2003; Gordon, 2001). Therefore, it is apparent that zero-tolerance strategies should be reserved only for the most severe aggressive and disruptive behaviors. Against this backdrop, we argue that students involved in bullying need to be taught relationship enhancement skills instead of being ostracized and punished for their lack of skills.

REALISTIC INDIVIDUAL STRATEGIES

We also want to be realistic about the nature of students' ability to respond to bullying behaviors. Take, for example, this exchange with a third-grade female student:

> STUDENT: I see a lot of bullying on the playground.
>
> DR. SWEARER: Who does the bullying?
>
> STUDENT: It's mostly the fifth graders who pick on the first and second graders when they're passing each other at recess.
>
> DR. SWEARER: So, what could you do about the bullying that you see?
>
> STUDENT: Nothing.
>
> DR. SWEARER: Why not?
>
> STUDENT: Because if I tried to tell the fifth graders to stop it, then they'd just bully me instead.
>
> DR. SWEARER: Could you tell a teacher?
>
> STUDENT: That wouldn't help. They'd just say that I was tattling or they'd tell me to tell the student's teacher. They don't really care.

What is most concerning about this dialogue is that at a very young age children seem to learn that (1) there is nothing they can do about the bullying and (2) adults do not care. When we tell children that "tattling" is bad, we are basically shutting down a form of communication between adults and children. As adults, we want to help students combat these feelings of helplessness and hopelessness when dealing with bullying behaviors.

INDIVIDUAL CHARACTERISTICS AND BULLYING

Many students who are involved in bullying experience co-occurring psychological problems (Kaltiala-Heino et al., 2001). For example, students who are struggling with feelings of depression may be more likely to bully others because of a sense of hopelessness or worthlessness. A student who is being victimized may be more likely to experience symptoms of anxiety because of the fear of being bullied (Swearer, Song, et al., 2001). Accurate assessment of these psychological symptoms is the first step in figuring out how to design effective individual interventions for these students (Merrell, 2001). The school psychologist is an individual who is trained to administer and interpret a variety of psychological characteristics that are associated with bullying behaviors. Table 7.1 provides a list of measures that can be administered by a trained professional to assess areas in need of additional intervention. Often by treating the underlying problems (i.e., depression, anxiety, aggression, impulsivity, distorted thinking, and skills deficits), the bullying/victimization dynamic can be thwarted.

TABLE 7.1. Instruments to Assess for Psychological Problems Associated with Bullying/Victimization

Problem	Measure	Age range	Order information
Depression	Children's Depression Inventory (CDI; Kovacs, 1992)	7–17 years	Multi-Health Systems Inc. *www.mhs.com*
Depression	Beck Depression Inventory–II (BDI-II; Beck, Steer, & Brown, 1996)	13–80 years	Harcourt Assessment *harcourtassessment.com*
Anxiety	Multidimensional Anxiety Scale for Children (MASC; March, 1997)	8–19 years	Multi-Health Systems Inc. *www.mhs.com*
Aggression	Aggression Questionnaire (AQ; Buss & Warren, 2000)	9–88 years	Western Psychological Services *www.wpspublish.com*
Attention-deficit/ hyperactivity disorder; impulsivity	Conners' Rating Scales— Revised (CRS-R; Conners, 1997)	3–17 years	Multi-Health Systems Inc. *www.mhs.com*
Cognitive distortions	How I Think Questionnaire (HIT; Barriga, Gibbs, Potter, & Liau, 2001)	12–21 years	Research Press Publishers *www.researchpress.com*
Self-concept	Self-Perception Profile for Children (Harter, 1985)	Children > age 8	University of Denver, author
Social skills	Social Skills Rating System (SSRS; Gresham & Elliott, 1990)	3–18 years	Pearson *www.pearsonassessments. com*
Behavioral functioning	Behavior Assessment System for Children, Second Edition (BASC-2; Reynolds & Kamphaus, 2004)	2–21 years	Pearson *www.pearsonassessments. com*
Bullying; victimization	Swearer Bully Survey	Grades 3–12	*www.targetbully.com*
Bullying; fighting; victimization	UIUC Aggression Scales	Grades 4–12	E-mail: *espelage@uiuc.edu*
Bullying; victimization	Reynolds Bully Victimization Scales for Schools	Grades 3–12	PsychCorp *www.psychcorp.com*

INDIVIDUAL INTERVENTIONS TO HELP STUDENTS
INVOLVED IN BULLYING

Assess the severity of the CB in light of this

Use the data to inform practice"

The vital part of any assessment is to use the data to inform practice. In our data-based decision-making model, we want to use assessment information to help design individual interventions. It is also important to understand where the focus of the intervention should be and how interventions can be modified over time. That said, we will assume that the mental health issues and psychological aspects of the bullying phenomena will be assessed accurately by the school psychologist. It is our belief that, although it is beneficial to have a schoolwide bullying prevention agenda, this approach will not necessarily help all youth who are bullies, victims, or bully-victims. Many students are chronically victimized, and often the victimization occurs for many years without notice or intervention. These victims need individual attention if we are to quell the negative impact of their psychological distress. Without intervention, these students are at risk for developing clinical levels of depression, anxiety, and in some rare cases anger problems, contributing to a shift from a victim to a bully-victim. Many bullies also have significant mental health issues that if not dealt with can lead to delinquency or violence in other relationships outside of school. We know that the long-term prognosis for both students who bully others and students who are victimized is poor. Thus, intervention at the individual level for these students is critical.

Individual counseling and psychoeducational group counseling are both excellent ways to curb depression and anxiety, prevent suicidal ideation and attempts, and promote improved social and relational skills, self-esteem, and general well-being. Many techniques that are used by trained mental health practitioners can also be employed by parents, teachers, and administrators. What are key ingredients to the clinician–client relationship? It is simple really. Psychologists and clients are an effective dyad when there is trust, authenticity, genuineness, honesty, and open communication. Whatever the intervention modality (e.g., individual, psychoeducational), these healthy relationship ingredients have to be present before any good psychotherapeutic work can take place. In order to create these ingredients, there has to be a direct discussion with the students about the goal of the intervention, the expectations from both the student and the counselor/psychologist/facilitator, the guidelines for respectful interactions, and the consequences for any digressions. In many ways, prevention and intervention of bullying should mirror the components of healthy relationships.

Once this foundation is established, the work of reducing bullying/victimization can begin. It is important to recognize that depression and anxiety among children and adolescents do not present themselves as they might in adulthood. In fact, there is a tremendous amount of variety in how these mood symptoms are manifested. So it is best that adults abandon their own conceptualization of depression and anxiety. More specifically, depression can evidence itself as irritability and anger in one child, but it might emerge as sadness and withdrawal in another. Children and adolescents do not always have the cognitive capacity to articulate what they are feeling and thinking and, therefore, need to be trained in identifying and labeling a variety of emotions. To be able to identify and label emotions, children and adolescents need to be taught about the many emotions that exist.

Using technology in a positive way, we have used the emotion icons from instant messaging to introduce the different types of emotions to students. Movies and books (see Chapter 6) can also be used to understand and label emotions. The next step is to have the youth track their feelings and thoughts on a daily basis. We often provide youth with a worksheet and ask them to write down a particular event that happened during the day that was upsetting or distressing in some capacity. They are then asked to write about the event and indicate what they were thinking when it happened, what they were feeling, and how they reacted. As we continue to work, this assignment is extended to include examining the rationality or feasibility of their thoughts and feelings, challenging any distorted thinking, and trying out different emotions and interpretations. Goals of this type of cognitive-behavioral approach are to introduce youth to a wide range of emotions, to teach them that they can monitor and track their cognitions, to encourage them to challenge some of their negative or distorted thinking, and to understand that they way they think and feel about situations is related to the way in which they behave.

Anger management strategies are also important for all youth. In fact, we believe that all adults and children would benefit from a mandatory anger management training course with booster sessions throughout life. Given that anger is a significant predictor of bullying perpetration and other behavioral issues (Espelage et al., 2000), we feel strongly that youth need to have skills to manage anger. However, there are some ground rules with good anger management training. First, everyone reading this book has to understand that anger is a normal, not an abnormal, emotion. Second, it is okay to be angry. What is not okay is taking that anger out on others through bullying or being mean. Thus, parents and teachers should not punish youth for being angry; rather, they should encourage them to talk through their anger and to manage it, not be managed by it. It is never too early and it is never too often to train youth in anger management. Additionally, youth learn from adults around them how to manage their anger. All adults should conduct their own assessment of their anger management skills before they work with children and adolescents!

We do not want to send the message that youth will quickly develop the skills to manage their anger. It takes time, trial and error, mistakes, and consistent intervention. The greatest hurdle that we encounter is that youth often behave in reaction to their anger by becoming aggressive without even knowing that they are angry and having no idea of what triggered their anger. We do know is that all individuals have certain things that trigger their anger, but most individuals rarely sit down and make a list of them. As adults, what angers you? Is it a slow driver? Is it someone being disrespectful to another person? Do you get frustrated before you get angry? Adults will only be helpful working with youth on their anger management strategies if they understand and can talk about their own anger triggers. Having youth track their day-to-day interactions will uncover their anger triggers.

Parents and teachers need to also be vigilant observers of the situations that trigger anger in their students and their children. Incidents that trigger a student's anger are what we like to call "teachable moments," which allow for adults to engage in anger management instruction in real time. For example, a teacher is having the class work quietly on a math worksheet and walks through the rows to monitor progress and work with students who are having difficulty. She notices that David, who struggles with math, is getting stuck and throws a pencil. At this point, the teacher goes over to David and asks him what he is feeling; he responds by saying he is mad and not good at math. Because this teacher encourages her students to speak openly about emotions, she asks him how he might manage his anger. He reluctantly responds that he could try to slow down, take a deep breath, and ask for help. These teachable moments occur in hallways, cafeterias, and playgrounds, in the home, and in public. We encourage adults to be active anger management interventionists who consistently model direct expression of emotion, speaking out loud when frustrated and not engaging in negative banter about other adults or friends in front of children.

Targeted individual interventions should also include assessment and modification of attributions. Aggressive youth sometimes have what is called a hostile attribution bias that leads to them misinterpreting certain situations (Coie & Dodge, 1998). Take, for example, the following situation: A boy steps on the foot of another boy in a crowded hallway and quickly apologizes. An aggressive boy who was stepped on might conclude that the behavior was intentional and deliberate and would likely not accept the apology but instead would shove the kid. A nonaggressive boy would be more likely than the aggressive boy to accept the apology and move one. Thus, it would be important to address the hostile attribution bias that the first boy manifested. The cognitive activities described previously are fundamental in attribution training (i.e., changing the way students attribute cause in a situation).

Attribution training has been found to increase students' persistence to overcome a challenge when faced with adversity (Forsterling, 1985). A recent study in the area of bullying substantiated the importance of attribution retraining for victims of bullying and bully-victims (Kingsbury & Espelage, in press). Briefly, the study found that victimization among middle school students was associated with greater self-blaming attributions and subsequent depressed affect. More specifically, victims (and bully-victims) who blamed their victimization on their personality or the way they look had greater depressed affect than victims (and bully-victims) who attributed the victimization to external reasons (something wrong with bully perpetrator). These findings also held for males and females and across Latino(a), African American, and European American students. According to these results, intervention programs should focus on training victims and bully-victims to engage in less self-blaming attributions, and such changes in attributions will likely lead to engagement in more adaptive coping strategies. According to attribution theory, the most adaptive self-appraisals following a negative event are those perceived as internal, unstable, and controllable, akin to a behavioral self-blaming attribution such as "I was in the wrong place at the wrong time" (Graham & Juvonen, 1998).

In addition to working with youth to manage their anger, depression, and anxiety, we believe it is important to discuss with youth their perceptions of aggression and bullying. Many youth who are involved in bullying find that they are rewarded through popularity and high social status (Rodkin & Hodges, 2003). In fact, students who bully others report feeling good about themselves, and students with high social power who bully others are rated as more popular, well-liked, athletic, attractive, and both physically and relationally aggressive (Vaillancourt, Hymel, & McDougall, 2003). Thus, if bullying others begets power and success in the peer group and in school, we can see why these behaviors are so difficult to eradicate. There are often few opportunities for them to explore how their bullying behaviors as a bully or an assistant to the bully might impact the victims. Thus, a strategy

THE STEREOTYPED BULLY:

for curtailing bullying involvement is to promote empathy toward the victim in youth. This can be done through the use of movies, books, creative writing assignments, reflection papers, storytelling, and drawing. This type of empathy training will not be effective, however, if youth do not begin to value prosocial behavior. It is our role as adults to challenge students to understand that valuing violence will be problematic in the long term. This is a major hurdle in a society where children and adolescents' are bombarded with aggression, violence, and bullying in television reality and news shows, in video games, and in their homes. Before turning our attention to interventions that target the other levels of the social-ecological model (peers, family, school, and community), we share with the readers a unique individual intervention strategy for youth who are involved in bullying perpetration.

This intervention is called the Bullying Intervention Program (BIP; Swearer & Givens, 2006). It is an individual cognitive-behavioral intervention for use with students who bully others and includes many aspects that have been highlighted in this chapter. Consistent with research, the BIP foundationally rests on the assumption that the social and cognitive perceptions of students involved in bullying interactions are just as important as aggressive attitudes and behaviors. Too often, schools focus on the behaviors but do not address the social and cognitive dimensions that contribute to the onset and maintenance of bullying. The BIP was developed because we know that homogenous group interventions are not helpful for aggressive youth and in some cases can be detrimental (Dishion, McCord, & Poulin, 1999).

The BIP includes school counselors and school psychologists working one on one with students who bully others. It was developed as an alternative to expulsion and suspension for students who are involved in bullying. More specifically, a middle school principal found that the all too common approaches of in-school suspension, suspension, and expulsion were ineffective in reducing bullying behaviors among his students. This principal reached out to a university faculty member to try something different. This professor confirmed the principal's suspicion by providing information that zero-tolerance policies are not effective in curbing aggressive behaviors (Casella, 2003) and that expulsion is equally ineffective in reducing aggressive behavior (Gordon, 2001).

Thus, the BIP is an alternative to in-school suspension for bullying behaviors that has been implemented in several elementary and middle schools in Nebraska. Rather than punishing a student who bullies others with in-school suspension, parents are offered the alternative of enrolling the student into the BIP. Since we began writing this book, 25 students have completed the program with their parents' consent. The BIP is a 3-hour one-on-one cognitive-behavioral intervention session with a master's-level therapist. There are three components to the BIP: (1) assessment, (2) psychoeducation, and (3) feedback. A 1-hour assessment is conducted and includes measures of bullying, depression, anxiety, cognitive distortions, school climate, and self-concept (see Table 7.1). This is followed by a 2-hour psychoeducational informational session about bullying, including defining bullying, outcomes of bullying, and what is known about why kids bully. The students are then given a quiz to assess their understanding of the material presented and then they complete several activities from *Bully Busters* (D. A. Newman, Horne, & Bartolomucci, 2000). Finally, the therapist and the referred student watch a video about bullying (either the MTV video about bullying, *Respect for All* [*www.respectforall.org*], *Bully Dance* [*www.bullfrogfilms.com*], or *Stories of Us* [*www.storiesofus.com*]). There is then time for the students to reflect on their understanding of the material, and they are encouraged to relate the materials to their own experiences. A report is then generated that incorporates the results of the assessment and the therapist's observation of the student in the activities. Recommendations are also indicated at the end of the report. This report and recommendations are shared in a meeting with the student, the parents, and a representative from the school.

The 25 participants were in grades 3 through 8, ranged in age from 8 to 14 years, and were primarily (93%) of European American descent. Of these students, 46.7% reported they both bullied others and were bullied (bully-victims); 20% reported they bullied others (bully); 13.3% reported they observed bullying (bystander); 13.3% reported they were victimized only (victim); and 6.7% reported that they were not involved at all in bullying. Although there are no empirical data yet to support the efficacy of the BIP, it is in line with our recommendations to focus on working with students who bully others individually to address knowledge related to bullying, effects of bullying, and social and cognitive aspects of bullying. We are optimistic that more schools will opt for these types of intervention programs rather than continuing to suspend and expel students, which do not teach students healthy relationship strategies.

PEER INTERVENTIONS TO HELP STUDENTS INVOLVED IN BULLYING

Very little progress has been made in developing bullying prevention programs that address peer norms that promote bullying others; however, the research points to several ways in which teachers, parents, and school administrators can work to modify peer influence. A brilliant starting point is to recognize explicitly with kids that many of them are involved in bullying others even if they are not directly engaging in the teasing. That is, students can be assistants to other students who are bullying, or they could simply do nothing or walk away without helping the victim. When working with youth in bullying prevention, we have them identify what roles they have taken in bullying experiences. As this discussion unfolds, students learn very quickly how their behavior plays a role in maintaining and in some cases escalating a bullying situation. It is not surprising that students do not intervene and support the victim of a bullying situation for many obvious reasons, and these barriers need to be discussed directly with youth. Youth are quite fearful of the bully group turning on them and feel helpless when they see bullying taking place.

Given this reality, it is up to the adults in the school to create a climate in which students feel that intervening is safe. It is instrumental for the adults to determine which peer groups are participating in the majority of the bullying and to attempt to dismantle these peers either through individual intervention or discussions with the parents of those involved. It is also worthwhile to try to have a discussion with the bully group ringleader and see whether he or she might be able to channel his or her power into more prosocial ways. School administrators and teachers should use these ringleaders in positive leadership roles. For example, these students could be selected to mentor younger students (under supervision), and through these interactions they might begin to move toward more positive interactions.

Parents also play an important role in diminishing the power of peers by talking to their children about the roles they play in bullying others. We must note that, in our combined decades of experience, we have rarely had parents admit that their sons or daughters play a part in bullying other students. This is naïve and does not bring about changes in our schools, homes, and communities. The research data consistently indicate that even though many students acknowledge that their behaviors are wrong, they still contribute in many ways to the bullying in elementary and middle school. Parents should encourage their children to question the attitudes and behaviors that bully ringleaders espouse. They should refuse to go along with the bullying but should do so with an explanation about how it is hurtful toward the victim.

FAMILY INTERVENTIONS TO HELP STUDENTS INVOLVED IN BULLYING

Teachers and parents need to have an open dialogue if bullying prevention is to have a long-lasting impact. Parents need to examine what messages they are sending their kids about violence, aggression, and respectful behavior. Are parents modeling aggression or disrespectful behavior? Do parents engage in exclusionary behaviors? What type of video games do parents allow their kids to play? What kind of television shows are they allowed to watch? Research consistently demonstrates a relation between observing violence in the home and involvement of students in bullying. Thus, we can no longer ignore the fact that many of our students who bully others reside in families in which violence and aggression are accepted ways of solving problems, either among parents or siblings.

SCHOOL-LEVEL INTERVENTIONS TO HELP STUDENTS INVOLVED IN BULLYING

Teachers can also do a tremendous amount to curb bullying in schools, at least at the classroom level (Holt & Keyes, 2004). First, teachers have to recognize that bullying happens in the classroom at high rates, but it is sometimes so subtle that they might not always see it. Second, they need to recognize that they are typically not good at determining who is involved in the bullying dynamic. Research has found that teachers do a poor job of accurately identifying victims (Holt & Keyes, 2004) and often misidentify bully-victims. Third, teachers need to resist being defensive around these issues and recognize that bullying happens in most classrooms and in most schools. However, despite these challenges, we have learned how teachers can minimize bullying in their classrooms and, by extension, their schools.

Teachers should work collaboratively with students to establish classroom guidelines about respectful and disrespectful attitudes and behaviors. Guidelines should include the notion that bullying is not respectful behavior; if a student is being bullied, the other students will support each other to get the victim help, and students and the teacher work together to make all students feel a sense of belonging in the classroom. These guidelines are often posted in the room and referred to frequently when bullying and peer conflicts arise. Students and teachers should also determine what will happen when there are digressions from the guidelines. We are proponents of classroom meetings, where guidelines are reviewed, emotions are discussed, and adaptive problem-solving strategies are modeled (Doll, Zucker, & Brehm, 2004). Once this atmosphere is created, the teachers should select a bullying prevention program that focuses on what bullying is, the effects of bullying, and the various roles that students take in bullying. Teachers should also get to know the milieu of their classroom by determining who has high or low social status, who is left out, and who is seen as a leader. Cooperative groups should be used, but members should vary across disciplines to promote a variety of interactions among kids.

COMMUNITY AND SOCIETAL INTERVENTIONS TO HELP STUDENTS INVOLVED IN BULLYING

After many combined years of conducting bully research, sometimes we end the day thinking that if we could just change society then maybe we could prevent bullying. It is true that our children are growing up in a violent society where disrespectful behavior toward others is seen in movies, television programming, and video games. When we look at the research on the impact of violent video games and aggression, it points to a need to do something. When all empirical studies using meta-analytic techniques are reviewed,

Anderson and Bushman (2001) found that viewing of violent video games was associated with increased aggressive behavior, thoughts, and affect; increased physiological arousal; and decreased prosocial (helping) behavior. Thus, it is imperative for adults to regulate and limit video game use and to have direct conversations with youth about the reality of the video games.

We also believe that communities need to work with schools, parents, and other organizations to forge an agenda to prevent bullying. The website associated with the national anti-bullying campaign (*www.stopbullyingnow.hrsa.gov*), supported and maintained by the U.S. Department of Health and Human Services, is a wonderful resource for community and school members to start their own campaign. The campaign, called *Stop Bullying Now!: Take a Stand, Lend a Hand*, provides schools and administrators with information on best practices in bullying prevention and intervention. Community organizations and schools can go to this site and download camera-ready print public service announcements and use them in newsletters or magazines. TV and radio commercials can be ordered for communities as well. Finally, posters can be reproduced and placed in public areas in an effort to promote a commitment to a community-supported bullying-prevention campaign.

CONCLUSIONS AND RECOMMENDATIONS

While we understand the tremendous pressures that schools face, we hope that school personnel and education stakeholders will take into account the data, which indicate that punishment-based strategies are not effective in reducing bullying behaviors. Individual assessment and intervention are vital components to effective bullying prevention and intervention. In fact, when we look at the data that have found that school bullying programs produced nonsignificant outcomes (Smith, Schneider, Smith, & Ananiadou, 2004) or only modest positive outcomes (Merrell, Gueldner, Ross, & Isava, 2008), we urge school personnel to carefully examine their bullying policies and practices. Providing individual support, restructuring peer groups, creating home–school partnerships (Cowan, Swearer, & Sheridan, 2004), creating school–community partnerships (Cowan & Swearer, 2004), and modeling healthy social relationships have the best chances of eradicating bullying from our schools and communities.

CASE EXAMPLE: SHELIA—A SIMPLE SOLUTION

A difficult situation often occurs when a student reports a bullying situation that was not witnessed by a teacher or administrator. Some school personnel tell us that their school has a policy of "If I don't see it, there's nothing I can do about it!" Policies like this serve to support and increase bullying behavior. Of course, students who bully others are not going to do so right under the watchful eye of an adult! This difficulty is highlighted by a situation that occurred recently in a high school classroom. Shelia was a slightly overweight adolescent who had a history of mild developmental delays. She had excelled in school through extreme hard work and was mainstreamed in all regular education classes. Although she had made generally good academic progress, she struggled socially. She was not always aware of students teasing her, but the teasing and name calling started increasing in one particular class. Every day two girls who sat on either side of Shelia would whisper degrading remarks to her in class. They also began asking her about her sex life and other inappropriate questions to embarrass Shelia. Shelia was not very assertive and was very uncomfortable going to the teacher given the nature of the comments.

Shelia had a very close relationship with her mother and reluctantly shared the nature of the situation with her mother. Shelia's mother called the teacher and told him what had been going on in his classroom. She asked that the other students be moved, and she was told that he could not do that because he did not actually hear them saying anything inappropriate. He did offer to move Shelia to the front of the classroom. However, Shelia viewed that as punishing her and had difficulty understanding why she was in trouble.

Thoughts about Shelia's Case

After a joint meeting with the teacher, the principal, and the mother, the teacher talked with the two girls and told them that they would be moving seats. He told them that he had overheard some negative comments so that they would not blame Shelia for getting them in trouble. This simple move ended the problem as they did not have access to Shelia and they were given the message that adults had overheard the comments and were watching them.

FOLLOW-UP QUESTIONS

1. As an adult, do you create a climate where students can come and talk with you? Or do you put them off by saying, "That's tattling" or "I didn't see anything, so there's nothing I can do." How do you help students problem solve?

2. Students who feel badly about themselves are vulnerable to being bullied. What strategies are in place in your school that help students find their strengths?

3. In this case, the bullying stopped when the girls who were doing the bullying were moved and when they were given the message that adults are watching. Adults are instrumental in creating the climate where bullying is reduced. What do you do to reduce the likelihood that bullying can occur?

4. Shelia's mother spent a good deal of time talking with the teacher and the principal. What would have happened had Shelia's mother not had the time or cared enough to go to the school? Who in your school advocates for kids who don't have this kind of family support?

8

The Impact of Technology on Relationships

A CHANGING WORLD

Computers, cell phones, instant messaging (IM), iPods, and computer games are commonplace in the lives of children and adolescents. When we were children, like many of the readers of this book, we played outside for hours upon hours and engaged in many creative activities that did not involve technology. We built bike ramps and tree forts and created entire "worlds" with our neighborhood friends. On summer nights, we only came back to the house when the sun was starting to set. Do kids still play outside, left to use their imagination, to fill the long summer days? Or are parents so concerned about their children's safety that their children are only allowed to be involved in structured and highly supervised activities? Or do they spend their time inside listening to their iPods, playing their video games, or chatting with their Internet friends?

Indeed, computers are a fixture in American households. Approximately 71% of U.S. households have Internet access according to a 2007 National Technology Scan by Parks Associates. A study by Nielson//NetRatings (2004) found that 77% of kids between the ages of 2 and 17 had Internet access, more than any other age group. Almost half of households surveyed (49%) reported that at least one child uses the Internet regularly, and by their teen years, three of four are online regularly (National School Boards Foundation, n.d.). Pew Internet (2005b) reported that 87% of U.S. teenagers (ages 12–17) currently use the Internet, representing approximately 21 million youth. Of those, approximately 11 million teens go online on a daily basis.

But what are they doing while they are online? A recent census report found that children and adolescents (ages 3–17) access the Internet at home most often for online gaming and next most often for working on homework assignments (U.S. Census Bureau News, 2005). The most popular types of online games are ones that involve trivia and puzzles. A rapidly growing number of teenage Internet users are being drawn to online social networking utilities such as Facebook and MySpace. Both are social networking websites offering an interactive network of friends, personal profiles, blogs, photos, and music. MySpace uses the music industry as their hook, offering fans, artists, and musicians the opportunity to connect with each other. Facebook is considered a safer networking community and has become the number one site for posting photos in the United States, with more than 8.5 million photos uploaded daily.

Statistically, MySpace is the most popular, with more than 70 million active users (Mashable, 2007). A Forrester Research report (2006) found that nearly 80% of youth between the ages of 12 and 17 years use MySpace at least weekly. Facebook is not as vast, with just over 30 million members, but membership is growing swiftly. During the past year, Facebook membership among youth under the age of 18 increased by 250%, whereas MySpace membership decreased by 30% (Mashable, 2007). The increase in Facebook membership was likely due to the developers' deliberate expansion beyond college student membership in September 2006. And MySpace users are apparently getting older. Mashable (2007) reports that teens accounted for 25% of users in August 2005 but currently only represent 12% of the audience. Later in this chapter we give parents, teachers, and administrators information about monitoring youth's MySpace and Facebook accounts.

IM also remains a popular form of online communication for youth. A recent Pew Internet and American Life Project (2008) study reports that although e-mail is still used by youth, the preferred modality of communication is IM. The study indicated that 75% of teens between the ages of 12 and 17 years used IM. Of these, 48% report using it at least every day. This study found that youth send more than just text through IM; 50% of those using IM have sent links to articles or websites and 45% have used it to send photos or documents.

Although it is clear that the Internet has become a popular place for kids to connect, cell phones remain a coveted medium. A recent Itracks survey (Mobiledia, 2005) found that one half of teens surveyed said they would rather have their TV privileges than their cell phone use restricted, and 27% indicated they would prefer to have web access or use of iPods limited rather than have their cell phones taken away. U.S. Cellular reported that about 60% of U.S. teenagers own a cell phone and spend an average of 1 hour a day on it, the same amount of time they spend on homework (CMCH Mentors for Parents and Teachers, 2007). Most teens get their first cell phone by the age of 15 years, and many 13-year-old children have cell phones (CMCH Mentors for Parents and Teachers, 2007). Cell phone companies are now marketing to even younger children with brightly colored, kid-friendly phones with easy-to-use features. According to the market research conducted by the firm Yankee Group, 54% of 8- to 12-year-olds will have their own cell phones within the next 3 years. In fact, the Walt Disney Company has been marketing Disney-themed cell phones to this age group since 2005 (*Washingtonpost.com*, 2005).

The latest craze in cell phone usage is text messaging; 936 billion text messages were sent in 2005, according to a Gartner study (2006). Gartner predicts this number will reach 2.3 trillion by 2010. Interestingly, Branding Unbound (2006) reports that the fastest growing group of texters is adults between the ages of 45 and 64 years. In a 2006 survey conducted by Cingular Wireless, nearly 50% of parents reported that their children introduced them to texting and 63% of parents reported it had improved communication with their child. According to a texting tutorial released by Cingular Wireless (2006) and clinical psychologist Ruth Peters, text messages are a way "to arm yourself with information and simultaneously raise your esteem in your children's eyes." Taking advantage of how teens prefer to communicate Century Council, an organization dedicated to prevent underage drinking and driving, encourages parents to use text messages on prom nights as a creative way to encourage their children to make wise decisions (Century Council, 2007).

THE NEGATIVE SIDE OF TECHNOLOGY

Generally, many would agree that the Internet has changed the world in numerous positive ways. The Internet allows individuals to stay in contact with their families and friends who might be overseas or across the United States. Health-related Internet sites permit users to access information and support for a variety of issues from determining the symptoms of depression to finding a support group for parents with children with ADHD. Children, adolescents, and adults also seek out, in some cases, their primary sources of support through networking sites and virtual worlds. These environments are social in many ways, despite not involving face-to-face interactions. Thus, these social environments are not immune to the various negative interactions that are encountered in schools, workplaces, families, and neighborhoods. However, what is, in fact, the potentially most disturbing outcome of excessive Internet use is the inability for children and adolescents to learn adequate social skills. These environments do not necessarily provide opportunities for children to learn how to navigate interpersonal relationships.

Before discussing the recent research on the intersection of technology and aggression, it is important to clarify the term that is often seen in the popular media: *cyberbullying* (Kowalski, Limber, & Agatston, 2008). Cyberbullying includes a multitude of types of aggressive online acts, and the following synonyms can be found in the literature and popular press: ebullying, electronic bullying, cyberviolence, digital bullying, electronic harassment, online harassment, and so on. A recent definition of cyberbullying posited by Ybarra and Mitchell (2004b) is "intentional and overt act of aggression toward another person online."

Cyberbullying has received a great deal of recent attention, mainly due to the tragic events surrounding a young girl's suicide as a result of cyberbullying. The alleged perpetrator, Lori Drew, the suburban St. Louis mother who allegedly helped create a fictitious person's MySpace account was indicted on Thursday, May 15, 2008 ("The 'MySpace suicide' trial," 2008). She convinced a friend of her daughter's, 13-year-old Megan Meier, that Megan was chatting with a boy who was interested in her. In October 2006 Megan hung herself after receiving cruel and hurtful messages from Lori Drew, allegedly posing as "Josh." This story, Jessica Haffer's story, and countless other stories must be a wake-up call to all of us that bullying, in all forms, can have disastrous consequences.

For the purpose of this chapter, the terms *Internet aggression* and *sexual solicitation* are used in our discussion of the detrimental effects of technology on relationships. Both Internet aggression (again, sometimes referred to as harassment or cyberbullying) and unwanted sexual solicitation are causing great concern among parents, teachers, and children and adolescents. Internet aggression can be categorized into types similar to those of face-to-face aggression: verbal, emotional, threatening, and social forms. Internet aggression includes, for example, rumors and rude or other harassing behaviors online. Studies have found that 10 to 33% of youth between the ages of 11 and 19 have been the target of aggression/bullying online (Finn, 2004; Patchin & Hinduja, 2006), and more than 15% of youth reported being perpetrators of such behaviors (Patchin & Hinduja, 2006). Additionally, 15% of youth had been targeted by unwanted sexual solicitation in a year on the Internet, including being asked to talk about sex, perform a sexual act, or provide personal sexual information against the youth's will (Ybarra & Mitchell, 2004a).

WHO IS INVOLVED?

In comparison to school-based aggression and bullying, the research on Internet aggression and sexual solicitation is in its infancy. Thus, there are many questions that remain about the characteristics of children/adolescents involved and how those involved vary across sex, race, age, and other characteristics. Ybarra and Mitchell (2004a) found that perpetrators of Internet aggression were more likely to be older youth and young males and females engaged in Internet aggression at equal rates. In contrast, some investigations implicate females as being perpetrators more often than males (Willard, 2007), but a recent study by Li (2006) reported males as perpetrators more often than females. It is evident that the discrepancies are due, in fact, to the lack of consensus of what constitutes Internet aggression, the use of different definitions and methods of data collection, and inherent sampling bias introduced with the use of online surveys.

Very few investigations have focused on how race plays out in the prevalence of online aggression. Although Internet use across ethnicity/racial groups overall differs very little, it appears that 40% of all bloggers are people of color (Pew Internet, 2005a). Tynes, Reynolds, and Greenfield (2004) explored incidences of racial comments in adolescent online chat rooms. They argued that racially based hate comments appear to be quite prevalent in these chat rooms and are more common in unmonitored sites where White and non-White groups experience hate comments equally. It is obvious that not much can be said about how race/ethnicity plays out with respect to online aggression, and even less can be said about the interaction among race/ethnicity, sex, class, and sexual orientation until more research is conducted.

Ybarra and colleagues are leading the field in helping paint a picture of the perpetrators of Internet aggression (Ybarra, 2004; Ybarra & Mitchell, 2004a, 2004b). The Internet holds a central place in the lives of Internet aggression perpetrators. Ybarra and Mitchell (2004a) reported that online aggression perpetrators were more likely to access the Internet more days per week in comparison to nonaggression Internet users. Online perpetrators report that their time spent on the Internet is very important, they report little parental supervision, and they consider themselves Internet experts. For example, an adolescent told us that she had her own website and one time someone pretended to be her and wrote "a bunch of stuff" about other people. This required an understanding of how to manipulate access to a website. Willard (2007) is also helping to understand predictors of those youth who might become involved as online aggressors. She has found that online aggression perpetrators are quite sophisticated in their technical skills (Willard, 2007). Online aggression perpetrators also appear to have experienced being a target of physical bullying at school more compared with nonaggressive online youth (Ybarra & Mitchell, 2004b). When online aggression perpetrators are asked why they engage in such behaviors, their responses mirror what is found in school-based research. Roughly 50% of online aggression perpetrators indicate that they do it "for fun" and 20% do it to teach the target a lesson (Patchin & Hinduja, 2006).

Much more is known about the Internet aggression targets. According to the Pew Internet and American Life Project report published in 2006, one third of students reported being targets of postings of personal communications for public viewing, rumors online, or threatening communication directed toward them. Ybarra (2004) found that targets reported using the Internet primarily for communication rather than for other purposes, and it appears that youth who create their own websites are at greater risk for victimization (Pew Internet & American Life Project, 2008). Similar to perpetration, males and females appear to be Internet aggression targets at equal rates in some studies (Ybarra, 2004), whereas females are found to be more common targets in other studies (Pew Internet & American Life Project, 2008). Only additional, solid empirical investigations of online behaviors will inform how sex influences involvement. For example, it is important to consider the amount of time youth use the Internet and how that increases their risk for online victimization. More specifically, Ybarra (2004) reported that more hours of Internet use increased the odds of victimization for females but not for males. It also appears that online victims are more likely to be managing clinical levels of depression (Finkelhor, Mitchell, & Wolak, 2000).

These high depression rates might be explained in part by recent research suggesting that experiences of victimization at school are associated with experiences of victimization and perpetration online. More specifically, youth who have been targets of bullying at school are more likely to engage in online aggression perpetration of others through the Internet (Ybarra, Espelage, & Mitchell, 2007; Ybarra & Mitchell, 2004b; Ybarra, Mitchell, Wolak, & Finkelhor, 2006). Similar to the bully-victims being overrepresented in the population of U.S. school shooters (Vossekuil et al., 2002), victims at school appear to seek retaliation by targeting their perpetrator online because seeking revenge at school would not be allowed. Alternatively, Willard (2007) has documented that targets of online aggression have sought out revenge at school when they were able to identify their perpetrators. Willard (2007) argued that this form of revenge often came in the form of physical aggression.

Aggression perpetration and victimization are not static roles within schools, with many children and adolescents taking on different roles at the same time or moving between categories (Love, Swearer, Lieske, Siebecker, & Givens, 2005). We discussed this issue in Chapter 1, and it appears that this movement between roles holds true for youth who use the Internet. Youth appear to assume multiple roles, including aggression perpetrators and victims at the same time (Ybarra, 2004). Much like the school-based literature on bully-victims, where they have the worse mental health outcomes, online aggressor/victims are found to have higher drug usage, lower school commitment, and more depression than youth who are uninvolved or take on only one role (Ybarra & Mitchell, 2004a, 2004b). They also tend to use the Internet more often than other groups of youth and report being monitored by their parents less often (Ybarra & Mitchell, 2004a). Males and females occupy this role equally, but they tend to be older youth (Ybarra & Mitchell, 2004a). A study by Ybarra et al. (2007) found a strong association between youth involved in online aggression perpetration and online sexual solicitation perpetration. This study also showed significant relations among online aggression perpetration and higher levels of relational, physical, and sexual aggression at school.

DO ONLINE PERPETRATORS AND VICTIMS KNOW EACH OTHER?

Face-to-face bullying and aggression leave no mystery as to who is involved. Indeed, some Internet aggression involves direct comments in which harassing messages or information is sent specifically from one person to another where the identities are known. Also, sometimes specific aggression comments are sent via Internet messaging or posted on web-boards. More recently, web-based surveys have been created to defame individuals by conducting polls about their behaviors (e.g., sexual behavior, attraction level), and in some cases pictures are modified to humiliate or embarrass the victims. Despite these types of

online aggression, much of the Internet aggression unfolds in an environment of anonymity, secrecy, avatars, and unidentifiable e-mail addresses, websites, and screen names. Given these characteristics, it is not surprising that few victims know who is directing the aggression toward them and, even less surprising, that the majority of online aggression perpetrators know their targets (Ybarra, 2004; Ybarra & Mitchell, 2004a, 2004b).

DOES ONLINE AGGRESSION MIRROR THE GROUP PROCESS LIKE SCHOOL BULLYING?

Much has been written in recent years about the fact that school-based bullying is often perpetrated by groups of kids and that kids socialize one another to bully their peers (see Chapter 3). We know that students who bully others have high levels of moral disengagement (Hymel, Rocke-Henderson, & Bonanno, 2005), and this ability to disengage might be even more heightened for students who engage in cyberbullying since technology affords the perpetrators a perceived level of anonymity. Willard (2007) recognizes the importance of exploring the extent to which groups of kids are gathering at one computer to engage in online aggression against other youth. She argues that some forms of online aggression are somewhat analogous to the "crank call." It is not clear how often this is happening among U.S. youth. However, it is recommended that parents place computers within community areas of their homes to prevent this type of group aggression from occurring. Put more directly, we suggest that parents DO NOT allow their children to have computers in their bedrooms.

WHAT EFFECT DOES ONLINE AGGRESSION INVOLVEMENT HAVE?

Studies consistently indicate that the majority of youth who use the Internet are not frequently involved in Internet aggression or sexual solicitation, either as a perpetrator or as a victim. However, for those who are involved, serious psychosocial costs are documented. For example, for both types of victimization, about one third of youth who were targeted reported feeling very or extremely upset about these experiences (Ybarra et al., 2006, 2007). With the potential to cause distress and widespread public humiliation (Strom & Strom, 2005), online aggression has a negative impact on individuals. Among those who are involved, however, a multitude of psychosocial problems are apparent, including substance use; involvement in offline victimization and perpetration of relational, physical, and sexual aggression; delinquent peers; a heightened anger disposition; and poor emotional bond with caregivers (Ybarra, 2004). This is especially true for youth who are involved both as perpetrators and victims of both Internet aggression and sexual solicitation (Ybarra et al., 2007). This small group of youth has emerged as an especially important group for adolescent health professionals to be aware of, identify, and treat or refer into services immediately.

WHAT DO KIDS DO WHEN THEY EXPERIENCE TECHNOLOGICALLY BASED AGGRESSION?

We have spent a lot of time recently talking to kids about what they do when they experience Internet and cell phone aggression. A consistent view that is held among youth is that they feel that technologically based aggression is worse than school-based aggression. Generally, kids feel that Internet aggressors are cowards because they do not have the courage to look at their victims face to face.

Kids have both simple and unique ways to deal with Internet aggression. For example, one girl told us that she was being sent threatening IMs from someone she did not know. Instead of getting upset, she added a friend to the conversation and then the aggression stopped. Students have also blocked the perpetrator. Another student indicated she was being sent threatening messages and other abusive text messages, and she just asked her mother to help get her cell phone number changed. An 8-year-old, when asked how he handled Internet aggression, remarked that he just turned off the computer. A 12-year-old girl told of being in a chatroom and feeling uncomfortable with some questions about her sexual interests. She indicated that she told others in the chatroom immediately and the individual never returned to that site.

WHAT CAN ADULTS DO?

The good news is that many kids told us that they felt very comfortable telling their parents about what was happening online. However, it appears that technologically based aggression is not going away. Some interventions are simple. Parents, teachers, and administrators need to talk with their kids about the responsible and respectable use of technology. Parents should not purchase their children cell phones until they understand this and the consequences of engaging in Internet or online aggression. As you recall from the beginning of this chapter, adolescents fear having their computer, cell phone, or iPod taken away from them. They should understand it is a privilege to have these things, which can be taken away.

Also, adults need to educate themselves about what is happening in the online world. We recommend that parents, teachers, and administrators spend some time learning about the websites that kids are visiting. Parents should be a friend in their children's social networks. Parents should have access to their children's MySpace account and to their e-mail accounts. We reiterate that the computers in the homes should be located outside of children's bedrooms. Certainly, kids will need some quiet area if they are working on school papers, but this can be done in an office that can be monitored randomly by parents. MySpace offers parents "The Official Parent and Family Guide to Understanding Your Teen's Use of MySpace" (2007a), which also includes information for concerned teachers and school resource officers. In this guide, adults are introduced to MySpace and are taught how to (1) create an account, (2) contact MySpace, (3) discuss their child's profile, (4) use MySpace as a family, (5) protect their child online, (6) remove a false profile, and (7) remove the child's profile. Information on cyberbullying is also provided. MySpace also offers similar information for school administrators in a guide entitled "The Official School Administrator's Guide to Understanding MySpace and Resolving Social Networking Issues" (2007b). Facebook does not appear to offer such guides, but does have information on their websites for parents on how to manage and regulate their child's profile.

With respect to school involvement, many schools have developed policies that allow cell phone use only before and after school. Parents feel that is important that their children have cell phones, but there was a time when kids did not have cell phones and, for the most part, kids were safe. There is no reason for kids to have cell phones during school hours. Cell phone use during school hours is disruptive and interferes with academics. Parents need to also attend technology update workshops because just as quickly as parental controls are created, software is designed to circumvent the controls. Parents should also know where their children are spending time on computers. More specifically, if their children spend a lot of time at friends' homes, parents should talk to these other parents about computer monitoring.

School administrators need to train their teachers to understand technology and how it can be used for both prosocial and deviant motives. Teachers could incorporate Internet and online aggression into their curriculum wherever possible. Students need to be responsible and smart consumers of the Internet and technology. It is important to demonstrate that anything posted on the web is permanent and not necessarily accurate. Students need to know that content of text messages can be retrieved from cell phone companies, and in most cases anything posted on the web can be traced to an IP address and, therefore, to their computer.

CONCLUSION AND RECOMMENDATIONS

It is true that when armed with knowledge about technology, parents and adults can intervene in online aggression. However, as the case of Megan Meier illustrates, adults themselves are not immune from participating in online aggression. Clearly, more education and awareness about the detrimental effects of online aggression need to be disseminated (see Figure 8.1 for a book club activity to increase knowledge about cyberbullying). School personnel must have ongoing discussions with students and their parents about technology and online aggression, and parents need to monitor their children's cell phone and computer usage. Just as most parents do not allow their children to roam the streets unsupervised, parents should also not allow their children to roam cyberspace unsupervised.

CASE EXAMPLE: LEWIS

Lewis had always struggled with social interaction and peer relationships. He often felt disconnected from his peers and longed to be part of the group. While he struggled socially,

Book groups are great venues for staff, parents, and students to read a book about a certain topic and then discuss the issues raised in the book. In order to increase awareness about cyberbullying, we recommend creating a book group around the book, *Cyber Bullying: Bullying in the Digital Age*, by Robin Kowalski, Susan Limber, and Patricia Agatston. Malden, MA: Blackwell Publishing.

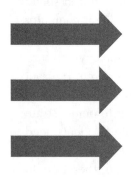

Step 1: Create a book club with 8–10 members.

Step 2: Read the book *Cyber Bullying*

Step 3: Discuss the book using the following questions as a guide:

1. What is cyberbullying?

2. What are the different modalitites for cyberbullying?

3. Why don't children tell about the bullying they experience?

4. How can you trace e-mails and text messages?

5. What role does the school play in stopping cyberbullying?

6. What legal options do victims have?

7. What should adults and students do if they witness cyberbullying?

8. Does your school policy include cyberbullying?

9. Does your school have staff training about technology?

10. What laws and policies apply to your state and school district?

FIGURE 8.1. Bookclub activity.

Lewis was a gifted athlete who excelled at sports. He focused most of his energy and time on baseball, and this became an area where he felt very comfortable and successful.

Within the baseball community, Lewis was well known. When he began high school, he finally felt as though he had found a good group of friends who were also good baseball players. He began spending increasing amounts of time with these peers. At first his parents were elated and relieved. They too had always hoped that Lewis would find his niche. However, Lewis's desire to fit in and have friends made him more vulnerable to becoming a victim of bullying. He tried so hard to be accepted that he overlooked many signs that this group of boys was not going to be good for him. They began with subtle put-downs and often made Lewis the butt of their jokes. This escalated into the group making more blatant negative remarks about him in public. Lewis was afraid to stand up for himself because he did not want to lose his "friends." He began doing whatever the group asked him to, including lying to his parents.

When Lewis tried to pull back, his peers became more controlling and rejecting. They were able to get Lewis to share his MySpace password with them, which led to the situation getting more out of control. Once Lewis had shared his password, the group of boys posted pictures of naked men on his page. They had changed Lewis's password so he could no longer access his own page, and he was unaware this was happening. Then one of the boys took Lewis's address book and e-mailed everyone, saying that he wanted to date them because he was gay.

When Lewis and his parents found out the extent of what was going on, they had some very difficult choices to make. Lewis was becoming increasingly depressed and withdrawn. His parents contemplated legal action, switching schools, and even moving. Lewis's father decided to call all of the parents of the boys involved before making any other decisions. He told them what had occurred and that he did not want their sons to have any contact with Lewis.

Lewis's parents experienced a variety of reactions from the other boys' parents. The parents of the boy they suspected to be the prime instigator of the Internet aggression were quite defensive. They said, "Well, boys just joke around." Lewis's father found that the other parents were more shocked and actually felt as though their children were coerced into following the leader.

The situation settled down, and Lewis decided to remain at his school and on the baseball team. He did not want to run from the situation. Lewis was very lucky to have a strong and supportive family. He also had a relationship with a psychologist prior to this situation getting out of control. He talked openly with his psychologist and with his parents, which helped him a great deal.

Lewis still feels anxious when he runs into his old friends but feels he has become a stronger person as a result of this experience. They talk occasionally, and Lewis sometimes feels like giving their friendships another try. However, he realizes that this would not be in his best interest. He is still looking for a good group of friends, but knows he will be fine even if he is not able to find that person or group.

FOLLOW-UP QUESTIONS

1. Children and adolescents often feel that their "good" friends will never hurt them, and it is common for youth to disclose their MySpace or Facebook passwords. Does your school teach students about the dangers of sharing passwords? As parents, do you have constant conversations with your children about Internet safety?

2. A popular elementary school toy and computer game, "WebKinz," socializes young children to the Internet. What do elementary schools and parents of elementary school students do to talk with elementary school children about the Internet. WebKinz is a fun, safe computer program and game. Might this socialize students into thinking that MySpace and Facebook are also fun and safe?

3. Where is your child's computer? We always tell parents, "*Never* let your child have a computer in his or her room." With the proliferation of wireless Internet and laptop computers, Internet access is easier than ever. How do you protect your children from Internet predators? Do you talk with your students about Internet predators?

4. We started this chapter by stating that when we were children we were out in the neighborhood playing and that parents today don't let their children roam around the neighborhood as freely. However, parents let their children open MySpace and Facebook webpages and allow them free Internet access. Isn't this the same as (or worse than) letting your children roam the streets?

9

Evaluating Your Efforts

We discussed several myths about bullying/victimization in Chapter 1, and in this chapter we restate those myths as realities about the bullying/victimization dynamic. We then present a compelling case example in which a middle school administration and staff used a data-based decision-making model to make some decisions about how to reduce bullying in their school. The purpose of this chapter is to help you think through how you will assess, prevent, and effectively intervene in bullying incidents and change the climate in your school.

We have, we hope, explained and demonstrated how complicated the bullying dynamic is among school-age youth. Eight facts about bullying/victimization, as explicated in this book, need to be acknowledged:

1. Bullying/victimization involves repeated, mean, aggressive behaviors.
2. All forms of bullying/victimization are damaging.
3. All individuals have the capacity to engage in bullying/victimization if the environment supports these behaviors.
4. Anti-bullying policies are a critical foundation for promoting an environment that does not support bullying/victimization.
5. Bullying/victimization is not a normal part of any developmental phase.
6. Bullying/victimization can be stopped when individuals choose not to engage in these behaviors.
7. Effective bullying prevention and intervention can be as simple as choosing to model and be in healthy social relationships.
8. Evaluation of bullying prevention and intervention is an ongoing effort that can be easily coordinated across the curriculum in any school.

NO MORE BULLYING ALLOWED!

To answer the fundamental question "What are the conditions that allow bullying/victimization to occur?," data need to be collected. As discussed in Chapter 6, every school should create an anti-bullying committee or a healthy school climate committee, and committee members can determine questions they would like to have answered. In Chapter 2, we provided a table of measures that can be used to assess social-ecological factors that might be contributing to the conditions that allow bullying/victimization. Once these surveys/measures are chosen, all students and staff in a school should be given the opportunity to answer the questions anonymously. In this way, school personnel will have data they can use to assess the scope of the bullying/victimization in their school and the conditions that support these behaviors. Figure 9.1 provides a checklist of evaluation guidelines that can be used to create a data-based decision-making climate in your school. In the rest of this chapter, we provide an example of how this data-based decision making can be put into action, including sample PowerPoint slides (Appendix 9.1).

Anywhere Middle School

The administrative staff and teachers in a very rural, impoverished district in the southeastern United States recognized that bullying/victimization was a part of the culture in their community. They told stories of high levels of abuse and neglect, drug and alcohol abuse, and truancy, as well as very low graduation rates. Given the larger pressing social issues in this community, at first glance, it might appear that bullying/victimization was the least of their problems. In fact, the staff in this school felt the opposite and that bullying was a problem they could tackle. They chose to conduct a schoolwide, anonymous survey. Their results and the manner of using data-based decision making are presented in the next sections.

Task 1: Establish an Anti-Bullying Evaluation Team

The district and school staff created an anti-bullying evaluation team that was composed of two administrators, two teachers, one school psychologist, two parents, and two students. This nine-member team met each month and decided to conduct a comprehensive schoolwide survey of bullying behaviors. They partnered with university researchers through the Target Bullying Survey and Intervention System: Ecologically Based Prevention and Intervention for Schools project (*www.targetbully.com*) to create a data-based decision-making climate. This multidisciplinary anti-bullying committee led the charge to engage in this process each spring.

Task 2: Meet and Brainstorm Questions

The anti-bullying evaluation team identified several areas of concern. They were concerned about mental health issues and wondered whether the students involved in bullying struggled with anxiety and depression. They also wanted to know whether bullying was equally present among boys and girls, where the bullying took place, if it was worse in the younger

Task	Timeline and Strategy
1. Establish an anti-bullying evaluation team. Team should include administrators, teachers, staff, parents, and students. All stakeholders should have a voice.	Summer before the start of each fall semester. Ideally, the team should include people who want to be on the team (not who are assigned against their will).
2. Meet and brainstorm questions that you would like to evaluate (i.e., "What is the scope of bullying in our school?," "What are the characteristics of the students who are doing the bullying?," "Do students feel bullied by teachers?," "Do teachers feel bullied by students?" etc.).	Early fall. Generate a list of questions and present questions to your district evaluation department (if you have one) or to critical stakeholders.
3. Research different assessment strategies and pick the one that will work best with your school and that will provide answers to your questions.	Early fall. Include math and/or statistics faculty in this decision. Consider partnering with university researchers so you collect usable data.
4. Decide when the best time to collect data will be. Make sure that data collection does not conflict with vacations, major school events, and testing.	Collect data in late fall before Thanksgiving or in the early spring semester. You want to collect data after peer groups have formed.
5. Decide whether or not you will collect data online or via paper and pencil.	Team members will need to examine the school's resources to determine the best way to collect data.
6. Consider approaching local business (i.e., Partners in Education) to obtain funding for data collections efforts.	School administrators can begin this process in the summer and establish partnerships for the upcoming school year.
7. Collect data at a consistent time each year. When students and teachers know that data are going to be collected, they look forward to the process and to receiving the results. One student wrote on a Bully Survey, "Thank you so much for asking my opinion each year. It means a lot."	Late fall or early spring every year. Consistency is *key* to establishing a maintaining a data-based decision-making climate.
8. Enter data either using an online survey program like Survey Monkey (*www.surveymonkey.com*) or SPSS (*www.spss.com*) or Excel (Microsoft Office).	As soon as the data are collected from all students or a representative sample of the majority of students in your school, develop a plan for entering the data. Partnering with university researchers, your district evaluation office, and/or math and statistics teachers is a great idea.
9. Analyze the data and develop a PowerPoint presentation that can be used to present the data to students, teachers, parents, and administration.	Use the sample PowerPoint presentation provided in Appendix 9.1 as a guide.
10. Generate ideas for bullying prevention and intervention based on your data.	Some of the most powerful prevention and intervention strategies come from looking at your own data and using your data to create lasting change.
11. Repeat every year to create a data-based decision-making climate in your school.	This process should be repeated each year.

FIGURE 9.1. Bullying evaluation guidelines.

grades, and the impact the bullying had on the students. A few questions asked were, What are the percentages of students involved in bullying others, being victimized, and observing bullying? What are students' attitudes toward bullying? Where is bullying occurring? What are students' comments about bullying? Given the other social stresses in this community and the sense that there were high levels of internalizing problems among their students, the committee also wanted to administer depression and anxiety screeners.

Task 3: Research Different Assessment Strategies

Based on the questions that the anti-bullying evaluation team created, they were interested in using a comprehensive survey to assess the experiences of the students who were bullied, the students who did the bullying, and the bystanders; attitudes toward bullying; teacher beliefs about bullying; and depression and anxiety. (The measures they chose to use are listed in Appendix 9.1 on slides 6–9.)

Task 4: Decide on a Time to Collect Data

In consultation with the school administration and looking at the school calendar, the team decided to collect data in late fall. They also wanted to leave time to have the data entered in SPSS (a statistical program; *www.spss.com*) so that the presentations of the data could be held in the spring semester.

Task 5: Decide on the Form of Data Collection

Given the financial constraints of this school and school district and the fact that they did not have adequate computer access for all students, they chose to collect data via paper-and-pencil assessments.

Task 6: Partner with Local Businesses and Foundations

To finance data collection, data entry, and data analysis, the district administration not only was very creative in using their safe and drug-free schools funds, but they also secured local donations from businesses and families for the data collection. Many community individuals are very interested in reducing bullying behaviors, and often community leaders can be approached to help with anti-bullying initiatives.

Task 7: Collect Data Consistently Each Year

The anti-bullying evaluation team decided to collect data in late fall (between Thanksgiving and the winter holiday) each year.

Task 8: Enter Data

The data were entered into SPSS and then analyzed in coordination with the math faculty at the school.

Task 9: Analyze the Data and Create a PowerPoint Presentation

Analyzing and presenting data can be a combined effort between math (graphing and analyzing data), English (writing the text), counseling (scoring psychological measures), and social studies (researching effects of bullying/victimization) departments. The presentation at this middle school was a coordinated effort between the administration and these departments. A sample PowerPoint presentation is shown in Appendix 9.1. Slides 1–5 set the stage for the presentation of the data. As can be seen in slide 4, the age ranges for each grade are fairly large. This was due to a number of students being held back and, therefore, being on the higher end of the age continuum. How might a 4-year age span in one grade support conditions for bullying behaviors? This was one of the questions that the anti-bullying team decided to tackle based on their data. This is an example of how data can influence policy. What can schools do to prevent students from being held back? As you will see in a later slide, bullying at this school predominately happens within each grade (as opposed to older students bullying younger students). Thus, the team learned some valuable information about the age demographic in each grade and learned that the large age range in each grade is contributing to the bullying behaviors at their school.

Slides 10–14 illustrate how students can be involved in learning about and calculating means, standard deviations, and percentages. Learning how to graph the data is another tool that can be taught and practiced in math classes. Additionally, bar graphs or pie charts are visually appealing and communicate the scope of the bullying experiences. As can be seen in slide 11, 29% of the students at this middle school reported being bullied daily or weekly during the current school year. Only 2.8% reported bullying others only, 20.1% reported engaging in both bullying others and being victimized, 22.1% reported observing bullying, and 24% reported not being involved in bullying. Thus, approximately 76% of students at this middle school reported involvement in the bullying/victimization dynamic.

Since this school was working with the Target Bullying research team, they were interested in comparison data (slides 15–18). What they learned was that, compared with another middle school in a different state, their student involvement in bullying/victimization was much higher and they needed to get their "not involved" numbers lower. Although this school was able to compare their data with data from a different school, another benefit of collecting data annually is that schools can then compare their data across years. When schools make a commitment to collect data annually, they have comparison data that they can use year after year to see whether their students' involvement in bullying decreases (hopefully!) over time.

Details about Bullying/Victimization

Information about gender (slide 19), where bullying occurs (slide 20), and the types of bullying students report (slide 22) is important in order to obtain a clear idea of the nature of the bullying/victimization in your school. As can be seen in these three slides, both boys and girls at this middle school were equally involved in bullying; most of the bullying took place in the hallway, classroom, bus, cafeteria, and gym; and much of the bullying was verbal. The connection between bullying/victimization and academic achievement is very important and one that is clearly documented in the literature (Fonagy, Twemlow, Vernberg, Sacco, & Little, 2005). In this school, 41% of the students reported that being bullied made it difficult for them to learn (slide 25). In many school districts, this academic connection is the information that is needed to support anti-bullying initiatives.

Qualitative and Quantitative Data

When possible, it is important to include open-ended questions in any surveys or assessments. Open-ended questions provide qualitative data that can be used to make your presentations interesting (slides 21, 23, 29, 33, 38–40). It is important, however, to make sure that you do not include student or staff names and that the comments that are included have been made by several students or teachers, not just one. You want to present themes so that individuals cannot be identified.

Who Is Doing the Bullying and Reasons for Being Bullied

These data suggest that verbal bullying is a major problem at this school and same-grade boys are doing much of the bullying (slide 24). These data illustrate the need to talk with students about the fact that verbal bullying is very damaging. It is our belief that consequences for verbal bullying should be the same as for physical bullying. It is also important to ask questions about why students feel they're bullied (slide 26). Issues such as being wimpy, being called gay, being called fat, and so on are important beliefs to assess and can provide a window into the school climate.

Relationship between Students and Adults

It is important to determine whether or not students are talking with the adults in their lives about bullying/victimization. One positive by-product of engaging in data-based decision making is that it communicates to students that the adults do care and they are asking for their opinion. Slide 27 indicates that 35% of students who report being bullied and 32% of students who report bullying others stated that the teachers did not know about the bullying. According to slide 28, the majority of students did not know how their teachers handled the bullying. These slides suggest that communication between students and teachers about bullying should be enhanced at this school.

Connection between Home and School

Given the other social issues in this community, the anti-bullying committee was interested in whether or not the students reported being bullied at home. There appeared to be some sibling bullying that was occurring for these students (slide 31). Of students who were bullied, 44% reported that their parents knew about this bullying. This is a positive indicator of parent–child communication. However, 33% reported that their parents did not know. The connection between home and school is an important one to assess and can be shared with parent and community groups.

Assessing Attitudes toward Bullying/Victimization

Examining support toward bullying is important. If the prevailing belief is that bullying/victimization is supported, this is a clear issue for intervention. It is not surprising that the students who are bullying others endorse supportive attitudes toward bullying; however, the fact that students who are also victimized (i.e., the bully-victims) have supportive attitudes toward bullying suggests that interventions to change beliefs about bullying would be important for these students.

Assessing Both Students and Teachers

This school was fortunate to have a staff who predominately felt that bullying/victimization was a problem (slides 34 and 35). Unfortunately, we have consulted with many schools where the students tell us that bullying is a problem and the staff tell us that bullying is not a problem. A difference of opinion between students and staff is an issue for intervention and suggests poor communication between adults and students.

Depression, Anxiety, and Bullying/Victimization

Although the students' scores were not clinically significant (slides 36 and 37), an important finding for the counseling department was that students who were victimized reported higher levels of anxiety than the other groups, and students who both bullied others and were victimized reported higher levels of depression than the other groups. This is consistent with the research on the relationship among depression, anxiety, and bullying/victimization and suggests that treatment for depression and anxiety for these students is warranted (Merrell, 2001).

Task 10: Generate Bullying Prevention and Intervention Strategies

Data tell a story about the bullying that is occurring in each school. Use the data to generate discussion and ideas for prevention and intervention (slide 41). Prevention efforts such as open communication between adults and students (slide 42) and modeling respectful behavior (slide 43) are vital. The data from the seventh-grade students suggest that intervention efforts should be geared toward the seventh graders (slide 44). Bullying at this school transcended gender lines and had a negative impact on learning (slide 45). Slide 46 targets specific interventions based on the locations where students reported being bullied. Enhancing adult–student interactions can help reduce bullying behaviors.

Task 11: Conduct Annual Evaluations

As we mentioned in Chapter 4, conducting yearly evaluations is important and also communicates that bullying/victimization is an important issue. Annual evaluations also let staff, parents, and students know that each year there is a mechanism for sharing their experiences and feelings about bullying/victimization. At the middle school described in this chapter, the staff and students had such a rewarding experience with the data-based decision-making model that they decided to collect data each year. The student council and school counseling staff use the PowerPoint slides for classroom presentations, the math teachers and students analyze the data and prepare the graphs, the social studies and English departments coordinate units on discrimination and bullying/victimization, and the data are shared with parent and community organizations. The experience has been transforming for the school and community.

FINAL THOUGHTS

We hope this book sparks a data-based call to action where school personnel and education stakeholders will engage in the process of collecting data annually about bullying, harassment, and discrimination in our nation's schools. We believe that when educators, parents, and students engage in understanding the conditions that foster bullying behaviors that they will then possess the necessary tools to end bullying/victimization in our schools and communities. We must all work compassionately and collectively to create healthy and positive relationships among all individuals. Only then will we have the potential to reduce 80% of the bullying behaviors to 0%.

Sample PowerPoint Presentation from Anywhere Middle School

Slide 1

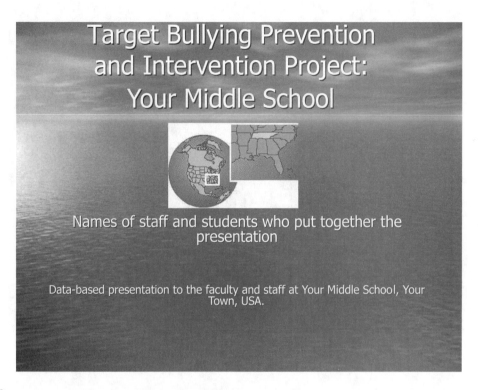

Slide 2

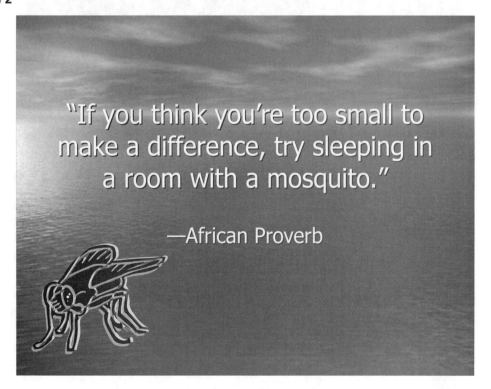

Slide 3

Slide 4

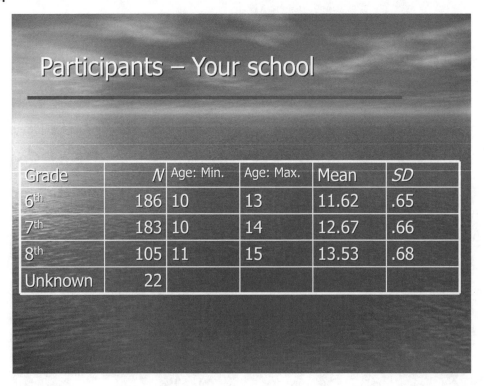

Grade	*N*	Age: Min.	Age: Max.	Mean	*SD*
6th	186	10	13	11.62	.65
7th	183	10	14	12.67	.66
8th	105	11	15	13.53	.68
Unknown	22				

Slide 5

Ethnicity of Participants

Ethnicity	N	%
Caucasian	454	91.5%
Latino/Hispanic	9	1.8%
Native American	4	0.8%
Other	3	0.6%
Black/ African American	1	0.2%
Did Not Report	29	8.8%

Slide 6

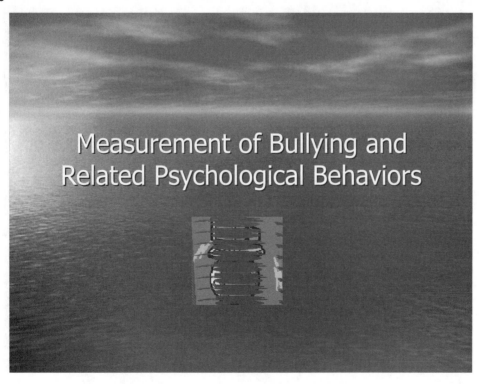

Measurement of Bullying and Related Psychological Behaviors

Slide 7

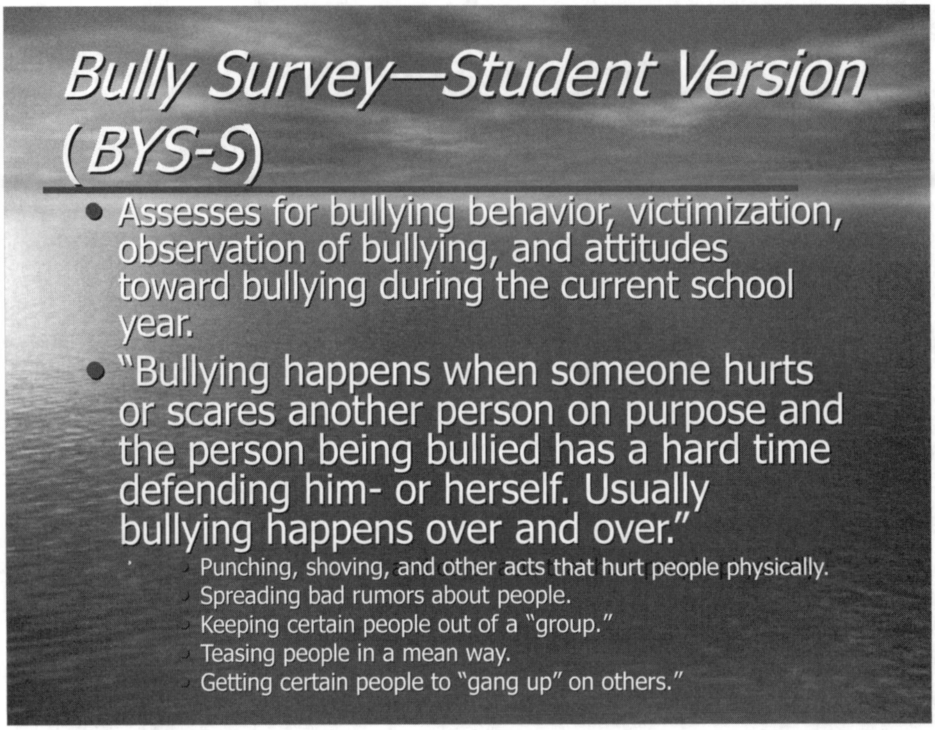

Bully Survey—Student Version (BYS-S)

- Assesses for bullying behavior, victimization, observation of bullying, and attitudes toward bullying during the current school year.
- "Bullying happens when someone hurts or scares another person on purpose and the person being bullied has a hard time defending him- or herself. Usually bullying happens over and over."
  - Punching, shoving, and other acts that hurt people physically.
  - Spreading bad rumors about people.
  - Keeping certain people out of a "group."
  - Teasing people in a mean way.
  - Getting certain people to "gang up" on others."

Slide 8

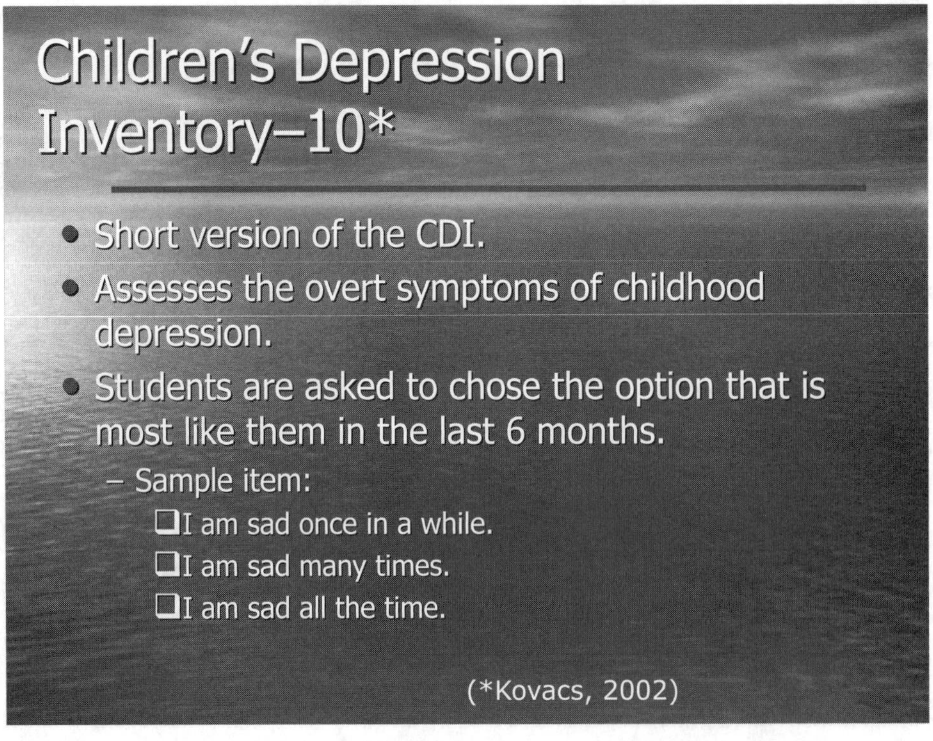

Children's Depression Inventory–10*

- Short version of the CDI.
- Assesses the overt symptoms of childhood depression.
- Students are asked to chose the option that is most like them in the last 6 months.
  - Sample item:
    - ❑ I am sad once in a while.
    - ❑ I am sad many times.
    - ❑ I am sad all the time.

(*Kovacs, 2002)

Slide 9

Multidimensional Anxiety Scale for Children—10*

- Shortened version of the MASC.
- Assesses major dimensions of anxiety in children ages 8 to 19.
- 10 items, 4-point Likert scale
  - Never true about me, Rarely true about me, Sometimes true about me, Often true about me
- Sample items:
  - —The idea of going away to camp scares me.
  - —I check to make sure things are safe.

(*March, 1997)

Slide 10

Involvement in Bullying: Descriptive Data

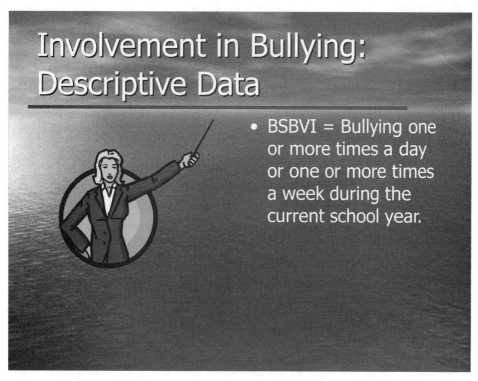

- BSBVI = Bullying one or more times a day or one or more times a week during the current school year.

Slide 11

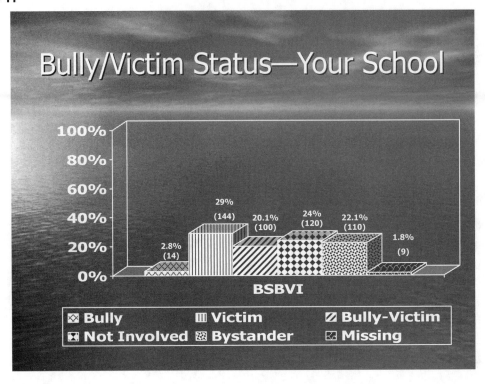

Slide 12

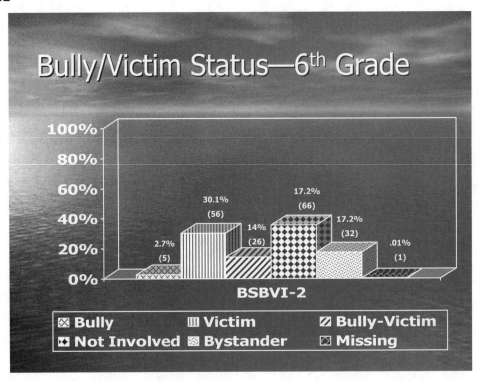

Slide 13

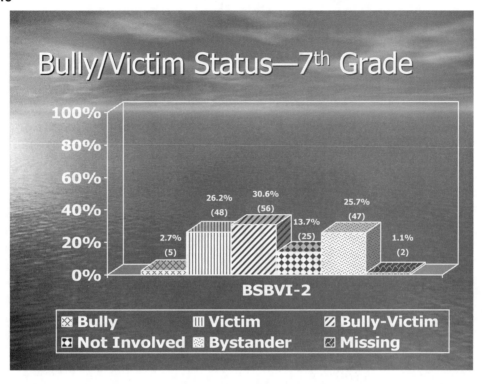

Slide 14

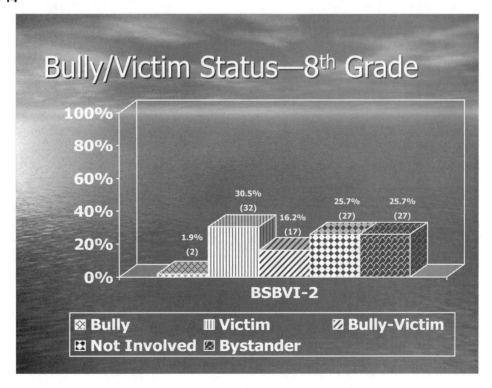

Slide 15

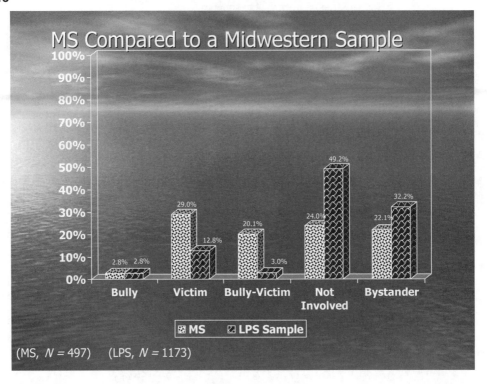

Slide 16

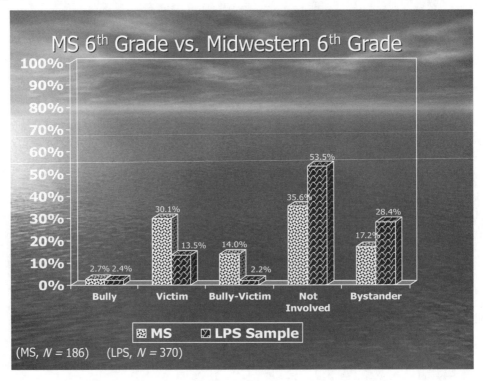

Slide 17

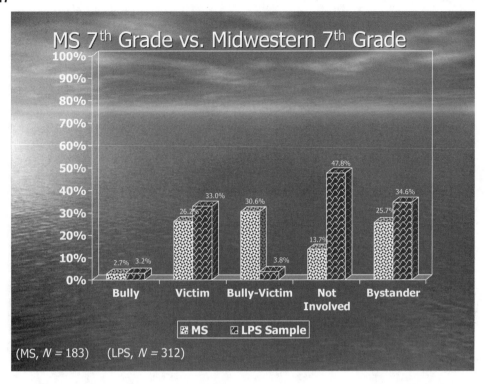

Slide 18

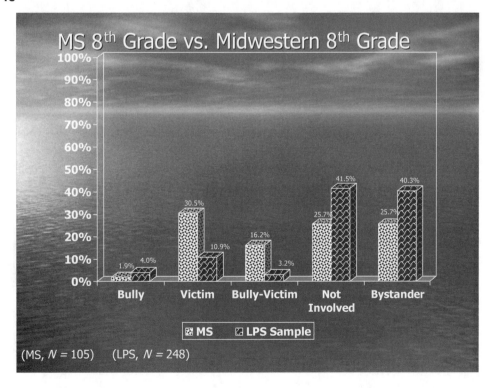

Slide 19

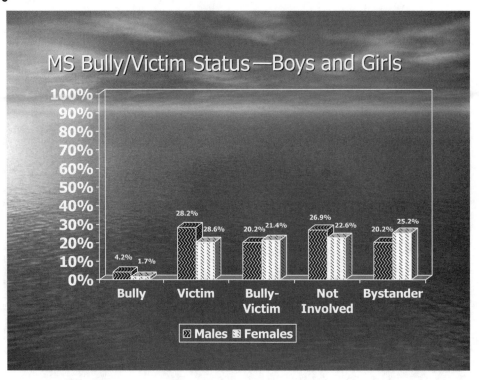

Slide 20

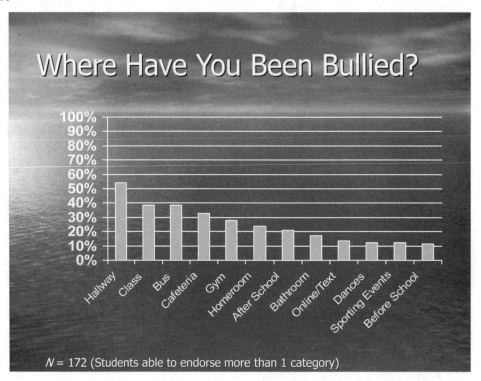

Slide 21

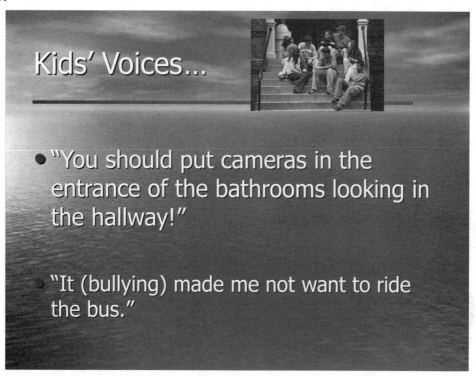

Slide 22

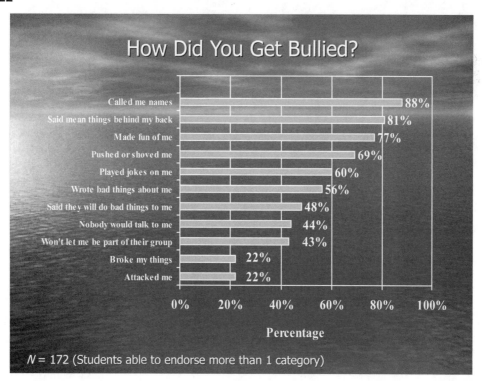

Slide 23

Kids' Voices...

- "They took the boy's belt off and beat him with it."

- "In the hallway they push the stuff out of my hands."

- "They (the bully) made them do nasty things."

Slide 24

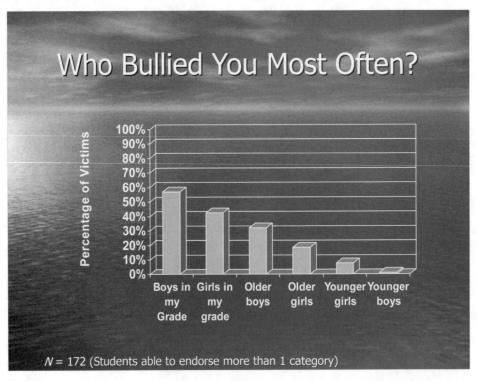

Who Bullied You Most Often?

N = 172 (Students able to endorse more than 1 category)

Slide 25

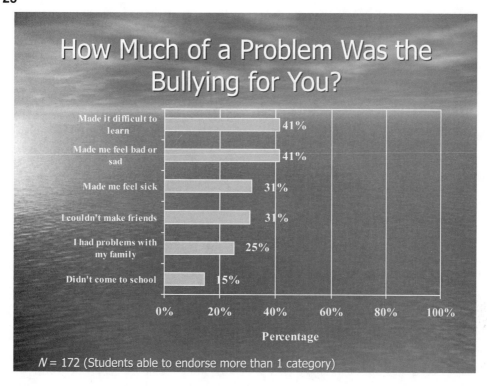

Slide 26

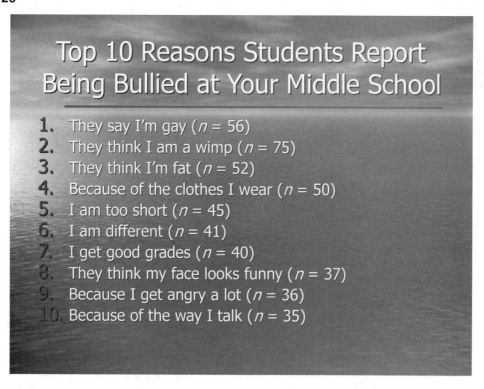

Slide 27

Did Teachers Know about the Bullying?

- 35% of Victims said "No" and 40% said "I don't know."

- 18% of Bystanders said "No" and 62% said "I don't know."

- 32% of Bullies & Bully-Victims said "No" and 36% said "I don't know."

Slide 28

How Do You Think Your Teachers and School Staff Took Care of the Bullying?

	Victims $N = 144$	Bystanders $N = 110$	Bullies & B-V $N = 114$
Very well	14%	7%	10%
Okay	20%	16%	13%
Bad	18%	13%	21%
I don't know	38%	57%	52%
Missing	10%	6%	4%

Slide 29

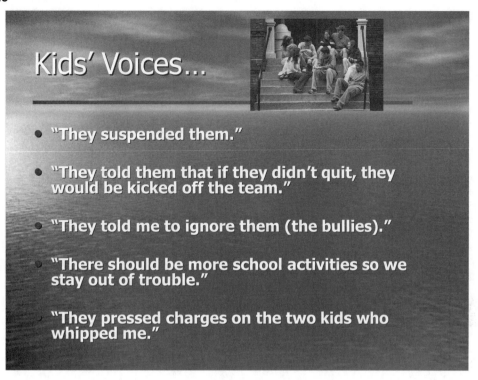

Slide 30

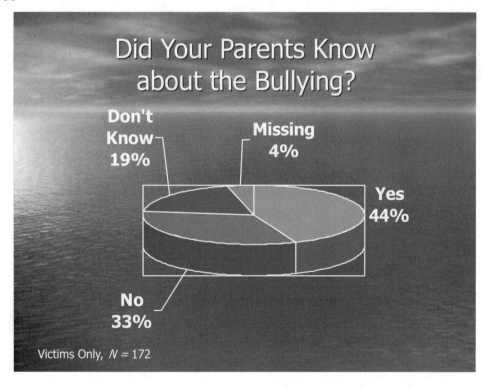

Slide 31

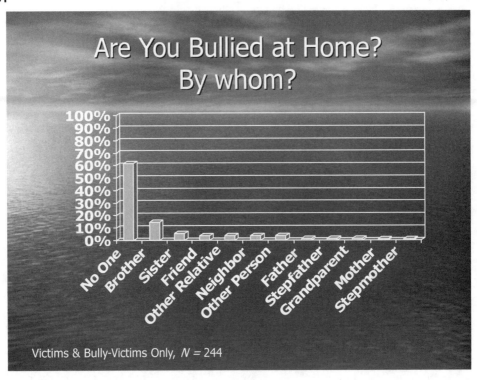

Slide 32

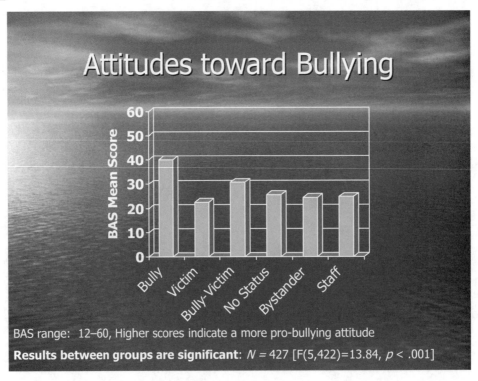

Slide 33

Kids' Voices...

- "I don't know why people bully other people. The bullies are just low on self-esteem."

- "Bullying shouldn't be able to happen."

- "The bullies should be punished."

Slide 34

Is Bullying a Problem at Your School?

- 62% of Students answered "Yes."

- 86% of Staff Members answered "Yes."

Slide 35

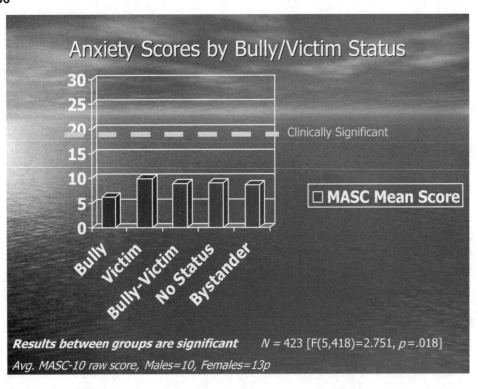

Should Schools Worry about Bullying?

- 76% of Students answered "Yes."

- 93% of Staff Members answered "Yes."

Slide 36

Anxiety Scores by Bully/Victim Status

Clinically Significant

☐ MASC Mean Score

Bully · Victim · Bully-Victim · No Status · Bystander

Results between groups are significant $N = 423$ [$F(5,418)=2.751$, $p=.018$]

Avg. MASC-10 raw score, Males=10, Females=13p

Slide 37

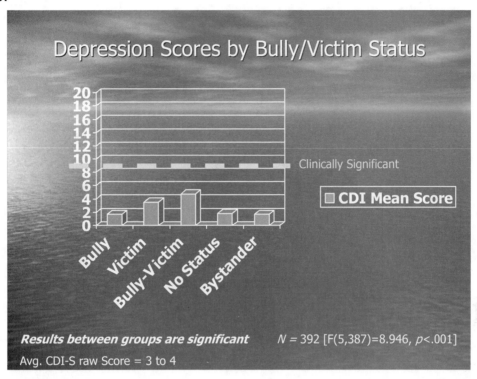

Slide 38

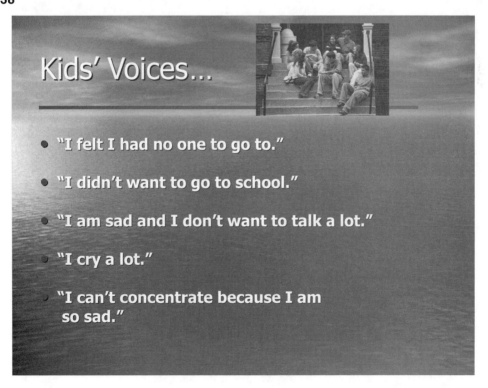

Slide 39

Teacher's Voices.....

- "He was labeled the class clown, but he was just trying to make jokes about himself before the others could."

- "The other children skip this boy in lunch line and he lets them because I think he is scared of them."

- "It seems to get worse every year to a more severe degree."

- "Bullying is a part of life, it can't be stopped, but we can teach students how to properly handle the situations."

Slide 40

Teacher's Voices.....

- "I took both students out in the hall, separately, and talked with them. The second time I heard it I made the bullying student serve a detention with me and made it very clear that one more time would be a Saturday scheduled detention."

- "Sent the 2 boys who were bullying the other boys to the office."

- "It is not a new problem. It went on when I was in school. Children are cruel. It should have been dealt with years ago."

Slide 41

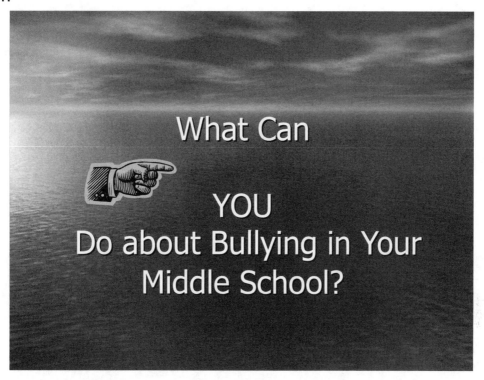

Slide 42

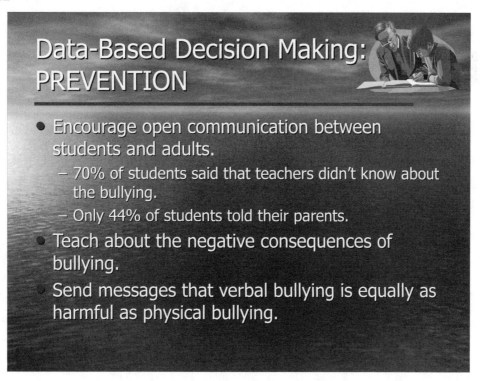

Slide 43

Data-Based Decision Making: PREVENTION

- What happens between 6th and 8th grades? An increase in the bully/victim dynamic, with 7th grade being the worst.
- There seems to be a same-grade bullying dynamic.
- You must get your "not involved" numbers higher!
- Model respectful behavior and develop consistent and enforceable consequences for bullying.

Slide 44

Data-Based Decision Making: INTERVENTION

- Only ¼ of students report not being involved in bullying...therefore, 75% of students at MS are involved in the bullying dynamic.
- The most not involved students are in 6th and 8th grades.
- What about those 7th graders? Highest bully-victim rates.
- Target 7th grade for interventions.

Slide 45

> # Data-Based Decision Making: INTERVENTION
>
> - Both boys and girls are equally involved in bullying at MS.
> - Bullying appears to happen among same-grade peers.
> - Bullying has a negative impact on learning.
> - Bullies and bully-victims held positive views of bullying. Bullying might be seen as positive—a sign of status and strength?

Slide 46

> # Top Five Places Where Bullying Occurs at MS
>
> - Hallway
>   - Increase hallway monitors.
> - Classroom
>   - Train all classroom teachers to identify bullying and to intervene consistently. Support teachers.
> - Bus
>   - Video cameras on buses? Train bus drivers.
> - Cafeteria
>   - Teachers should eat lunch with the students.
> - Gym
>   - PE teacher(s) must actively be involved in stopping bullying behaviors.

Slide 47

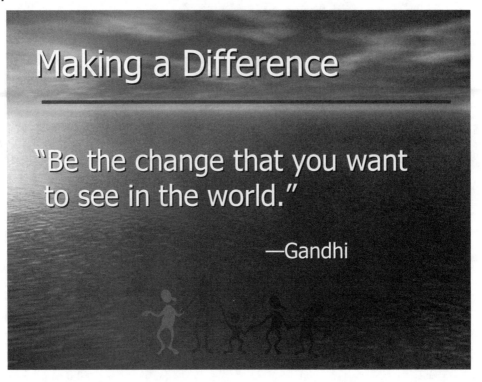

References

Alaska Session Laws 109. (2006).

American Association of University Women. (1993). *Hostile hallways: The AAUW survey on sexual harassment in America's schools* (Research Rep. No. 923012). Washington, DC: Harris/Scholastic Research.

American Association of University Women. (2001). *Hostile hallways: Bullying, teasing and sexual harassment in school.* Washington, DC: Author.

Americans with Disabilities Act, 42 U.S.C. § 12134 (2006).

Anderson, C. A., & Bushman, B. J. (2001). Effects of violent video games on aggressive behavior, aggressive cognition, aggressive affect, physiological arousal, and prosocial behavior: A meta-analytic review of the scientific literature. *Psychological Science, 12,* 353–359.

Anderson, C. A., & Bushman, B. J. (2002). Human aggression. *Annual Review of Psychology, 53,* 27–51.

APA Task Force on Zero Tolerance. (2007). Are zero tolerance policies effective in the schools?: An evidentiary review and recommendations. Retrieved July 10, 2008, from *www.apa.org/ed/cpse/zttfreport.pdf.*

Arizona Revised Statutes § 15–341 (2005).

Arkansas Department of Education. (n.d.). Recommendations for writing anti-bullying policies. Retrieved April 1, 2008, from *arkedu.state.ar.us/commendos/static/fy0203/attachments/Policy_Writing_Recs.doc.*

Astington, J. W., Harris, P. L., & Olson, D. R. (1988). *Developing theories of mind.* Cambridge, UK: Cambridge University Press.

Astor, R. A., Meyer, H. A., & Pitner, R. O. (2001). Elementary and middle school students' perceptions of violence-prone school subcontexts. *Elementary School Journal, 101,* 511–528.

Austin, S., & Joseph, S. (1996). Assessment of bully/victim problems in 8- to 11-year-olds. *British Journal of Educational Psychology, 66,* 447–456.

Baldry, A. C. (2003). Bullying in schools and exposure to domestic violence. *Child Abuse and Neglect, 27,* 713–732.

Baldry, A. C., & Farrington, D. P. (2000). Bullies and delinquents: Personal characteristics and parental styles. *Journal of Community and Applied Social Psychology, 10,* 17–31.

Barriga, A. Q., Gibbs, J. C., Potter, G. B., & Liau, A. K. (2001). *How I Think Questionnaire.* Champaign, IL: Research Press.

Batsche, G. M., & Knoff, H. M. (1994). Bullies and their victims: Understanding pervasive problem in the schools. *School Psychology Review, 23,* 165–174.

Beck, A. T., Steer, R. A., & Brown, G. K. (1996). *Manual for the Beck Depression Inventory–II.* San Antonio, TX: Psychological Corporation.

Berkowitz, L. (1993). *Aggression: Its causes, consequences, and control.* New York: McGraw-Hill.

Bjorklund, D. F., & Pellegrini, A. D. (2002). *The origins of human nature.* Washington, DC: American Psychological Association.

Borg, M. G. (1998). The emotional reactions of school bullies and their victims. *Educational Psychology, 18,* 433–443.

Boulton, M. J. (1992). Rough physical play in adolescents: Does it serve a dominance function? *Early Education and Development, 3,* 312–333.

Bowers, L., Smith, P. K., & Binney, V. (1994). Perceived family relationships of bullies, victims, and bully/victims in middle childhood. *Journal of Social and Personal Relationships, 11,* 215–232.

Bradshaw, C. P., Sawyer, A. L., & O'Brennan, L. M. (2007). Bullying and peer victimization at school: Perceptual differences between students and school staff. *School Psychology Review, 36,* 361–382.

Branding Unbound. (2006, December 18). Fastest growing segment of texters: 45- to 64-year-olds. Retrieved October 23, 2007, from *maverix.typepad.com/brandingunbound/2006/12/fastest_growing.html.*

Bronfenbrenner, U. (1977). Toward an experimental ecology of human development. *American Psychologist, 32,* 513–531.

Bronfenbrenner, U. (1979). Contexts of child rearing: Problems and prospects. *American Psychologist, 34,* 844–850.

Bukowski, W. M., Sippola, L. K., & Newcomb, A. F. (2000). Variations in patterns of attraction to same- and other-sex peers during early adolescence. *Developmental Psychology, 36,* 147–154.

Buss, A. H., & Warren, W. L. (2000). *Aggression Questionnaire: Manual.* Los Angeles, CA: Western Psychological Services.

Cairns, R. B., & Cairns, B. D. (1994). *Lifelines and risks: Pathways of youth in our time.* Cambridge, UK: Cambridge University Press.

California Department of Education. (n.d.). Sample policy for bullying prevention. Retrieved April 1, 2008, from *cde.ca.gov/ls/ss/se/samplepolicy.asp.*

Casella, R. (2003). Zero tolerance policy in schools: Rationale, consequences, and alternatives. *Teachers College Record, 105,* 872–892.

Center for the Study and Prevention of Violence. (n.d.). Colorado Association of School Boards sample policy on bullying. Retrieved April 1, 2008, from *www.colorado.edu/cspv/safeschools/bullying/bullying_casbpolicy.html.*

Century Council. (2007, April 13). Text message your teen on prom night. Retrieved October 23, 2007, from *www.centurycouncil.org/press/2007/pr2007–04–13.html.*

Christenson, S. L., & Sheridan, S. M. (2001). *Schools and families: Creating essential connections for learning.* New York: Guilford Press.

Cingular Wireless. (2006, August 29). Txt2Connect: Survey indicates text messaging improves parent–child communications. Retrieved October 23, 2007, from *www.prnewswire.com/mnr/cingular/25194/.*

Civil Rights Act of 1964, 42 U.S.C. § 2000d. (2006) ("Title VI").

Clinton, H. R. (1996). *It takes a village and other lessons children teach us.* New York: Simon & Schuster.

CMCH Mentors for Parents and Teachers. (n.d.). Cell phones. Retrieved October 23, 2007, from *www.cmch.tv/mentors/hotTopic.asp?id=70.*

Cohen, D., & Strayer, J. (1996). Empathy in conduct-disordered and comparison youth. *Developmental Psychology, 32,* 988–998.

Coie, J. D., & Dodge, K. A. (1998). Aggression and antisocial behavior. In N. Eisenberg (Ed.) & W. Damon (Series Ed.), *Handbook of child psychology: Vol. 3. Social, emotional and personality development* (5th ed., pp. 779–862). New York: Wiley.

Colorado Revised Statutes § 22-32-109.1 (2005).

Connecticut Public Acts 115 (2006).

Conners, K. (1997). *Conners' Rating Scales—Revised: Manual.* Tonawanda, NY: Multi-Health Systems.

Connolly, J., Pepler, D. J., Craig, W. M., & Taradash, A. (2000). Dating experiences of bullies in early adolescence. *Child Maltreatment: Journal of the American Professional Society on the Abuse of Children, 5,* 299–310.

County of Sacramento v. Lewis, 523 U.S. 833 (1998).

Cowan, R., & Swearer, S. M. (2004). School-community partnerships. In C. Spielberger (Ed.), *Encyclopedia of applied psychology* (Vol. 2, pp. 309–317). San Diego, CA: Academic Press.

Cowan, R., Swearer, S. M., & Sheridan, S. M. (2004). Home-School collaboration. In C. Spielberger (Ed.), *Encyclopedia of applied psychology* (Vol. 2, pp. 201–208). San Diego, CA: Academic Press.

Craig, W. M. (1998). The relationship among bullying, victimization, depression, anxiety, and aggression in elementary school children. *Personality and Individual Differences, 24,* 123–130.

Craig, W. M., & Pepler, D. J. (1997). Observations of bullying and victimization in the school yard. *Canadian Journal of School Psychology, 13*(2), 41–59.

Crick, N. R. (1999). "Superiority" is in the eye of the beholder: A comment on Sutton, Smith, and Swettenham. *Social Development, 8,* 128–131.

Crick, N. R., & Grotpeter, J. K. (1995). Relational aggression, gender, and social-psychological adjustment. *Child Development, 66,* 710–722.

Cunningham, N. J. (2007). Level of bonding to school and perception of the school environment by bullies, victims, and bully victims. *Journal of Early Adolescence, 27,* 457–478.

Curley v. Hill, 2000 U.S. Dist. LEXIS 16665 (S.D. Ind. 2000).

Davis v. Monroe County Board of Education, 526 U.S. 629 (1999).

Davis, M. H. (1983). Measuring individual differences in empathy: Evidence for a multidimensional approach. *Journal of Personality and Social Psychology, 44,* 113–126.

Demaray, M. K., & Malecki, C. K. (2002). The relationship between perceived social support and maladjustment for students at risk. *Psychology in the Schools, 39,* 305–316.

Demaray, T. R., & Malecki, M. K. (2003). Perceptions of the frequency and importance of social support by students classified as victims, bullies, and bully/victims in an urban middle school. *School Psychology Review, 32,* 471–489.

Dempsey, J. P., Fireman, G. D., & Wang, E. M. (2006). Transitioning out of peer victimization in school children: Gender and behavioral characteristics. *Journal of Psychopathology and Behavioral Assessment, 28*(4), 271–280.

DeShaney v. Winnebago County Department of Social Services, 489 U.S. 189, 197 (1989).

DeSouza, E. R., & Ribeiro, J. (2005). Bullying and sexual harassment among Brazilian high school students. *Journal of Interpersonal Violence, 20,* 1018–1038.

Dishion, T. J., McCord, J., & Poulin, F. (1999). When interventions harm: Peer groups and problem behavior. *American Psychologist, 54,* 755–764.

Dodge, K. A., & Coie, J. D. (1987). Social information processing factors in reactive and proactive aggression in children's peer groups. *Journal of Personality and Social Psychology, 53,* 1146–1158.

Dodge, K. A., Pettit, G. S., McClaskey, C. L., & Brown, M. M. (1986). Social competence in children. *Monographs of the Society for Research in Child Development, 51,* 1–85.

Doe v. Town of Bourne, 2004 U.S. Dist. LEXIS 10021 (D. Mass. 2004).

Doll, B., Zucker, S., & Brehm, K. (2004). *Resilient classrooms: Creating healthy environments for learning.* New York: Guilford Press.

Duncan, R. D. (1999). Maltreatment by parents and peers: The relationship between child abuse, bullying victimization, and psychological distress. *Child Maltreatment, 4,* 45–55.

Duncan, R. D. (2004). The impact of family relationships on school bullies and their victims. In D. L. Espelage & S. M. Swearer (Eds.), *Bullying in American schools: A social-ecological perspective on prevention and intervention* (pp. 227–244). Mahwah, NJ: Erlbaum.

Education Amendments Act of 1972, 20 U.S.C. § 1681 (2006) ("Title IX").

Endresen, I. M., & Olweus, D. (2001). Self-reported empathy in Norwegian adolescents: Sex differences, age trends, and relationship to bullying. In A. C. Bohart, C. Arthur, & D. J. Stipek (Eds.), *Constructive and destructive behavior: Implications for family, school, and society* (pp. 147–165). Washington, DC: American Psychological Association.

Eron, L. D., Huesmann, L. R., Dubow, E., Romanoff, R., & Yarnel, P. W. (1987). Aggression and its correlates over 22 years. In D. H. Crowell & I. M. Evans (Eds.), *Childhood aggression and violence: Sources of influence, prevention, and control* (pp. 249–262). New York: Plenum Press.

Espelage, D. L., Bosworth, K., & Simon, T. R. (2000). Examining the social context of bullying behaviors in early adolescence. *Journal of Counseling and Development, 78,* 326–333.

Espelage, D. L., & Green, H. D. (in press). Willingness to intervene in bullying episodes among middle school students: The role of empathy and peer-group membership. *Social Networks.*

Espelage, D. L., Green, H. Jr., & Wasserman, S. (2007). Statistical analysis of friendship patterns and bullying behaviors among youth. In L. Hanish & P. Rodkin (Eds.), *Peer social networks: New directions for child and adolescent development* (pp. 61–75). San Francisco: Jossey-Bass.

Espelage, D. L., & Holt, M. K. (2001). Bullying and victimization during early adolescence: Peer influences and psychosocial correlates. In R. Geffner & M. Loring (Eds.), *Bullying behaviors: Current issues, research, and interventions* (pp. 123–132). Binghampton, NY: Haworth Press.

Espelage, D. L., Holt, M. K., & Henkel, R. R. (2003). Examination of peer-group contextual effects on aggression during early adolescence. *Child Development, 74*(1), 205–220.

Espelage, D. L., Holt, M., Poteat, P., & VanBoven, A. (in press). Bullying in the schools. In J. Eccles & J. Meece (Eds.), *Schooling and development.* New York: Routledge.

Espelage, D. L., Mebane, S. E., & Adams, R. S. (2004). Empathy, caring, and bullying: Toward an understanding of complex associations. In D. L. Espelage & S. M. Swearer (Eds.), *Bullying in American schools: A social-ecological perspective on prevention and intervention* (pp. 37–61). Mahwah, NJ: Erlbaum.

Espelage, D. L., & Swearer, S. M. (2003). Research on school bullying and victimization: What have we learned and where do we go from here? *School Psychology Review, 32,* 365–383.

Espelage, D. L., & Swearer, S. M. (2004). *Bullying in American schools: A social-ecological perspective on prevention and intervention.* Mahwah, NJ: Erlbaum.

Farmer, T. W., Estell, D. B., Bishop, J. L., O'Neil, K. K., & Cairns, B. D. (2003). Rejected bullies or popular leaders? The social relations of aggressive subtypes of African American early adolescents. *Developmental Psychology, 39,* 992–1004.

Farmer, T. W., Leung, M. C., Pearl, R., Rodkin, P. C., Cadwallader, T. W., & Van Acker, R. (2002). Deviant or diverse peer groups? The peer affiliations of aggressive elementary students. *Journal of Educational Psychology, 94*, 611–620.

Feshbach, N. D., & Feshbach, S. (1982). Empathy training and the regulation of aggression: Potentialities and limitations. *Academic Psychology Bulletin, 4*(3), 399–413.

Finkelhor, D., Mitchell, K., & Wolak J. (2000). *Online victimization: A report on the nation's young people.* Alexandria, VA: National Center for Missing & Exploited Children.

Finn, J. (2004). A survey of online harassment at a university campus. *Journal of Interpersonal Violence, 19*, 468–483.

Flores v. Morgan Hill Unified School District, 324 F.3d 1130, 1134 (9th Cir. 2003).

Flouri, E., & Buchanan, A. (2003). The role of mother involvement and father involvement in adolescent bullying behavior. *Journal of Interpersonal Violence, 18*, 634–644.

Fonagy, P., Twemlow, S. W., Vernberg, E., Sacco, F. C., & Little, T. D. (2005). Creating a peaceful school learning environment: The impact of an antibullying program on educational attainment in elementary schools. *Medical Science Monitor, 11*, 317–325.

Forrester Research. (2007, July 11). NACTAS Q4 2006 youth media and marketing and finance online survey. Retrieved October 23, 2007, from *www.forrester.com/ER/Research/Survey/Excerpt/1,5449,535,00.html.*

Forsterling, F. (1985). Attributional retraining: A review. *Psychological Bulletin, 98*, 495–512.

Furlong, M. J., Morrison, G. M., & Greif, J. L. (2003). Reaching an American consensus: Reactions to the special issue on school bullying. *School Psychology Review, 32*, 456–470.

Gartner. (2006, December 13). Gartner highlights key predictions for IT organizations in 2007 and beyond. Retrieved October 23, 2007, from *www.gartner.com/it/page.jsp?id=499323.*

Georgia Code Annotated § 20-2-751.4 (2006).

Gordon, A. (2001). School exclusions in England: Children's voices and adult solutions. *Educational Studies, 27*, 69–85.

Graham, S., Bellmore, A. D., & Mize, J. (2006). Peer victimization, aggression, and their co-occurrence in middle school: Pathways to adjustment problems. *Journal of Abnormal Child Psychology, 34*, 363–378.

Graham, S., & Juvonen, J. (1998). Self-blame and peer victimization in middle school: An attributional analysis. *Developmental Psychology, 34*, 587–599.

Graham, S., & Juvonen, J. (2001). An attributional approach to peer victimization. In S. Graham & J. Juvonen (Eds.), *Peer harassment in school: The plight of the vulnerable and victimized* (pp. 49–72). New York: Guilford Press.

Gregory, K. E., & Vessey, J. A. (2004). Bibliotherapy: A strategy to help students with bullying. *Journal of School Nursing, 20*, 127–133.

Gresham, F. M., & Elliott, S. N. (1990). *Social Skills Rating System manual.* Circle Pines, MN: American Guidance Service.

Griffith, J. (1996). Relation of parental involvement, empowerment, and school traits to student academic performance. *Journal of Educational Research, 90*, 33–41.

Gruber, J. E., & Fineran, S. (2007). The impact of bullying and sexual harassment on middle and high school girls. *Violence Against Women, 13*, 627–643.

Hanish, L. D., Kochenderfer-Ladd, B., Fabes, R. A., Martin, C. L., & Denning, D. (2004). Bullying among young children: The influence of peers and teachers. In D. L. Espelage & S. M. Swearer (Eds.), *Bullying in American schools: A social-ecological perspective on prevention and intervention* (pp. 141–159). Mahwah, NJ: Erlbaum.

Harachi, T. W., Fleming, C. B., White, H. R., Ensminger, M. E., Abbott, R. D., Catalano, R. F., et al. (2006). Aggressive behavior among girls and boys during middle childhood: Predictors and sequelae of trajectory group membership. *Aggressive Behavior, 32,* 279–293.

Harter, S. (1985). *Manual for Self-Perception Profile for Children.* Denver, CO: University of Denver.

Hawker, D. S. J., & Boulton, M. J. (2000). Twenty years' research on peer victimization and psychosocial maladjustment: A meta-analytic review of cross-sectional studies. *Journal of Child Psychology and Psychiatry and Allied Disciplines, 41,* 441–455.

Hawkins, J. D., Catalano, R. F., & Miller, J. Y. (1992). Risk and protective factors for alcohol and other drug problems in adolescence and early adulthood: Implications for substance abuse prevention. *Psychological Bulletin, 112,* 64–105.

Hawley, P. H. (1999). The ontogenesis of social dominance: A strategy-based evolutionary perspective. *Developmental Review, 19,* 97–132.

Hawley, P. H., Little, T. D., & Rodkin, P. C. (2007). *Aggression and adaptation: The bright side to bad behavior.* Mahwah, NJ: Erlbaum.

Haynie, D. L., Nansel, T., & Eitel, P. (2001). Bullies, victims, and bully/victims: Distinct groups of at-risk youth. *Journal of Early Adolescence, 21,* 29–49.

Health Resources and Services Administration. (n.d.). *Best practices in bullying prevention and intervention.* Retrieved July 17, 2007, from *www.stopbullyingnow.hrsa.gov/HHS_PSA/pdfs/SBN_Tip_23.pdf.*

Henry, D., Guerra, N., Huesmann, R., Tolan, P., Van Acker, R., & Eron, L. (2000). Normative influences on aggression in urban elementary school classrooms. *American Journal of Community Psychology, 28,* 59–81.

Hirschi, T. (1969). *Causes of delinquency.* Berkeley: University of California Press.

Hodges, E. V. E., & Perry, D. G. (1999). Personal and interpersonal antecedents and consequences of victimization by peers. *Journal of Personality and Social Psychology, 76,* 677–685.

Hoffman, M. L. (2000). *Empathy and moral development: Implications for caring and justice.* New York: Cambridge University Press.

Holt, M., Finkelhor, D., & Kaufman Kantor, G. (2007). Hidden victimization in bullying assessment. *School Psychology Review, 36,* 345–360.

Holt, M., & Keyes, M. (2004). Teachers' attitudes toward teasing and general school climate. In D. L. Espelage & S. M. Swearer (Eds.), *Bullying in American schools: A social-ecological perspective on prevention and intervention* (pp. 121–139). Mahwah, NJ: Erlbaum.

Hoover, J. H., Oliver, R., & Hazler, R. J. (1992). Bullying: Perceptions of adolescent victims in the midwestern USA. *School Psychology International, 13,* 5–16.

Horne, A. M., Bartolomucci, C. L., & Newman-Carlson, D. (2003). *Bully busters: A teacher's manual for helping bullies, victims, and bystanders.* Champaign, IL: Research Press.

Howard, K. A., Flora, J., & Griffin, M. (1999). Violence-prevention programs in schools: State of the science and implications for future research. *Applied & Preventive Psychology, 8,* 197–215.

Huber, J. D. (1983). Comparison of disciplinary concerns in small and large schools. *Small School Forum, 4,* 7–9.

Huesmann, L. R., Eron, L. D., Lefkowitz, M. M., & Walder, L. O. (1984). Stability of aggression over time and generations. *Developmental Psychology, 20,* 1120–1134.

Hymel, S., Rocke-Henderson, N., & Bonanno, R. A. (2005). Moral disengagement: A framework for understanding bullying among adolescents. *Journal of Social Sciences, 8,* 1–11.

Indiana Code Annotated § 5-2-10.1-2 (Michie 2006).

Iowa Department of Education. (2007). Anti-bullying/anti-harassment sample policy. Retrieved April 1, 2008, from *www.iowa.gov/educate/content/view/942/1106*.

Juvonen, J., & Graham, S. (2001). Self-views versus peer perceptions of victim status among early adolescents. In J. Juvonen & S. Graham (Eds.), *Peer harassment in school: The plight of the vulnerable and victimized* (pp. 105–124). New York: Guilford Press.

K. M. v. Hyde Park Central School District, 381 F. Supp. 2d 343 (S.D.N.Y. 2005).

Kaltiala-Heino, R., Rimpelae, M., & Rantanen, P. (2001). Bullying at school: An indicator for adolescents at risk for mental disorders. *Journal of Adolescence, 23*, 661–674.

Kandel, D. B. (1978). Homophily, selection, and socialization in adolescent friendships. *American Journal of Sociology, 84*, 427–436.

Kasen, S., Berenson, K., Cohen, P., & Johnson, J. (2004). The effects of school climate on changes in aggressive and other behaviors related to bullying. In D. L. Espelage & S. M. Swearer (Eds.), *Bullying in American schools: A social-ecological perspective on prevention and intervention* (pp. 187–210). Mahwah, NJ: Erlbaum.

Kasen, S., Cohen, P., & Brook, J. S. (1998). Adolescent school experiences and dropout, adolescent pregnancy, and young adult deviant behavior. *Journal of Adolescent Research, 13*, 49–72.

Kasen, S., Johnson, J., & Cohen, P. (1990). The impact of school emotional climate on student psychopathology. *Journal of Abnormal Child Psychology, 18*, 165–177.

Kaufman, P., Chen, X., Chandler, S. P., Chapman, K. A., Rand, C. D., & Ringel, M. R. (1998). *Indicators of school crime and safety* (NCES 98-251/NCJ-172215). Washington, DC: U.S. Government Printing Office.

Kaukiainen, A., Bjorkqvist, K., Lagerspetz, K., Osterman, K., Salmivalli, C., Rothberg, S., et al. (1999). The relationships between social intelligence, empathy, and three types of aggression. *Aggressive Behavior, 25*, 81–89.

Kellam, S. G., Ling, X., Merisca, R., Brown, H. C., & Ialongo, N. (1998). The effect of the level of aggression in the first grade classroom on the course and malleability of aggressive behavior into middle school. *Development and Psychopathology, 10*, 165–185.

Kingsbury, W., & Espelage, D. L. (in press). Self-blaming attributions as mediators between victimization and psychological outcomes during early adolescence. *European Journal of Educational Psychology*.

Koch, R. (1998). *The 80/20 principle: The secret to success by achieving more with less.* New York: Doubleday.

Kochenderfer, B. J., & Ladd, G. W. (1996a). Peer victimization: Cause or consequence of school maladjustment? *Child Development, 67*, 1305–1317.

Kochenderfer, B. J., & Ladd, G. W. (1996b). Peer victimization: Manifestations and relations to school adjustment in kindergarten. *Journal of School Psychology, 34*, 267–283.

Kovacs, M. (1992). *Children's Depression Inventory.* New York: Multi-Health Systems.

Kowalski, R. M., Limber, S. P., & Agatston, P. W. (2008). *Cyber bullying: Bullying in the digital age.* Malden, MA: Blackwell.

Li, Q. (2006). Cyberbullying in schools: A research of gender differences. *School Psychology International, 27*, 157–170.

Limber, S. P. (2006). Peer victimization: The nature and prevalence of bullying among children and youth. In N. E. Dowd, D. G. Singer, & R. F. Wilson (Eds.), *Handbook of children, culture, and violence* (pp. 331–332). Thousand Oaks, CA: Sage.

Limber, S. P., & Small, M. S. (2003). U.S. laws and policies to address bullying in schools. *School Psychology Review, 32*, 445–455.

Loeber, R., & Dishion, T. (1984). Boys who fight at home and school: Family conditions influencing cross-setting consistency. *Journal of Consulting and Clinical Psychology, 52*(5), 759–768.

Love, K. B., Swearer, S. M., Lieske, J., Siebecker, A. B., & Givens, J. (2005, August). *School climate, victimization, and anxiety in male high school students.* Poster presented at the 113th Annual Convention of the American Psychological Association, Washington, DC.

Maine School Management Association. (n.d.). Sample policy. Retrieved April 1, 2008, from *www. maine.gov/education/bullyingprevention/management.rtf.*

March, J. S. (1997). *Manual for the Multidimensional Anxiety Scale for Children.* Toronto: Multi-Health Systems.

Mashable. (2007, July 11). MySpace losing high schoolers to facebook? Retrieved October 23, 2007, from *mashable.com/2007/07/11/myspace-losing-to-facebook.*

Mass. Gov. (n.d.). Promoting civil rights and prohibiting harassment, bullying, discrimination, and hate crimes: Sample policy for Massachusetts school districts. Retrieved April 1, 2008, from *www.mass.gov/Cago/docs/Community/SSI/Children_CivilRightsPolicyHighlights.rtf.*

McFadyen-Ketchum, S. A., Bates, J. E., Dodge, K. A., & Pettit, G. S. (1996). Patterns of change in early childhood aggressive-disruptive behavior: Gender differences in predictions from early coercive and affectionate mother-child interactions. *Child Development, 67*(5), 2417–2433.

Mehrabian, A. (1997). Relations among personality scales of aggression, violence, and empathy: Validational evidence bearing on the Risk of Eruptive Violence Scale. *Aggressive Behavior, 23,* 433–445.

Mehrabian, A., & Epstein, N. (1972). A measure of emotional empathy. *Journal of Personality, 40,* 525–543.

Menesini, E., Sanchez, V., Fonzi, A., Ortega, R., Costabile, A., & Feudo, G. L. (2003). Moral emotions and bullying: A cross-national comparison of differences between bullies, victims, and outsiders. *Aggressive Behavior, 29,* 515–530.

Merrell, K. W. (2001). *Helping students overcome depression and anxiety: A practical guide.* New York: Guilford Press.

Merrell, K. W., Gueldner, B. A., Ross, S. W., & Isava, D. M. (2008). How effective are school bullying intervention programs?: A meta-analysis of intervention research. *School Psychology Quarterly, 23,* 26–42.

Mikle, J. (2005, December 8). Harassed student's court win upheld. *Asbury Park Press.*

Miller, P. A., & Eisenberg, N. (1988). The relationship of empathy to aggressive and externalizing/ antisocial behavior. *Psychological Bulletin, 103,* 324–344.

Mo. SB 894 (enacted July 10, 2006).

Mobiledia. (2005, August 30). Survey finds 50% of teens prefer cell phones to TV. Retrieved October 23, 2007, from *www.mobiledia.com/news/35398.html.*

Moeller, T. G. (2001). *Youth aggression and violence: A psychological approach.* Mahwah, NJ: Erlbaum.

Moffitt, T. E. (1993). Adolescent-limited and life-course-persistent anti-social behavior: A developmental taxonomy. *Psychological Review, 100,* 674–701.

Mohr, A. (2006). Family variables associated with peer victimization: Does family violence enhance the probability of being victimized by peers? *Swiss Journal of Psychology, 65,* 107–116.

MySpace. (2007a, August 6). The official parent and family guide to understanding your teen's use of MySpace. Retrieved June 9, 2008, from *creative.myspace.com/cms/SafetySite/documents/ MySpaceParentGuide.pdf.*

MySpace. (2007b). The official school administrator's guide to understanding MySpace and resolving social networking issues. Retrieved March 30, 2008, from *instech.knox.k12tn.net/training/www/documents/myspaceadministratorguide71007-1.pdf.*

The "MySpace suicide" trial. (2008). *Los Angeles Times.* Retrieved May 22, 2008, from *www.latimes.com/news/local/la-me-myspace16-2008may16,0,3642392.story.*

Nansel, T. R., Haynie, D. L., & Simons-Morton, B. G. (2003). The association of bullying and victimization with middle school adjustment. *Journal of Applied School Psychology, 19,* 45–61.

Nansel, T. R., Overpeck, M., Pilla, R. S., Ruan, W. J., Simmons-Morton, B., & Scheidt, P. (2001). Bullying behavior among U.S. youth: Prevalence and association with psychosocial adjustment. *Journal of the American Medical Association, 285,* 2094–2100.

National School Boards Foundation. (n.d.). Safe & smart: Research and guidelines for children's use of the Internet. Retrieved October 23, 2007, from *www.nsbf.org/safe-smart/full-report.htm.*

Nebraska Unicameral. (2008). 100th Legislature, 2nd session. Legislative Bill 205. Retrieved April 1, 2008, from *uniweb.legislature.ne.gov/FloorDocs/Current/PDF/Final/LB205.pdf.*

New Jersey Statutes Annotated § 18A:37-15 (2006).

Newman, D. A., Horne, A. M., & Bartolomucci, C. L. (2000). *Bully busters: A teacher's manual for helping bullies, victims, and bystanders.* Champaign, IL: Research Press.

Newman, R. S., Murray, B., & Lussier, C. (2001). Confrontation with aggressive peers at school: Students' reluctance to seek help from the teacher. *Journal of Educational Psychology, 93*(2), 398–410.

Nielson//NetRatings. (2004, March 18). Three out of four Americans have access to the Internet, according to Nielsen//Net ratings. Retrieved October 23, 2007, from *www.nielsen-netratings.com/pr/pr_040318.pdf.*

No Child Left Behind Act of 2001, Public Law No. 107-110 (2001).

Nordhagen, R., Nielson, A., Stigum, H., & Kohler, L. (2005). Parental reported bullying among Nordic children: A population-based study. *Child: Care, Health and Development, 31,* 693–701.

Ohio Department of Education. (2007). *Anti-harassment, anti-intimidation or anti-bullying model policy.* Columbus, OH: Author.

Oliver, R., Oaks, I. N., & Hoover, J. H. (1994). Family issues and interventions in bully and victim relationships. *School Counselor, 41,* 199–202.

Olweus, D. (1993a). *Bullying at school: What we know and what we can do.* New York: Blackwell.

Olweus, D. (1993b). Bully/victim problems among schoolchildren: Long-term consequences and an effective intervention program. In S. Hodgins (Ed.), *Mental disorder and crime* (pp. 317–349). Thousand Oaks, CA: Sage.

Olweus, D. (1994). Bullying at school: Long-term outcomes for the victims and an effective school-based intervention program. In L. R. Huesmann (Ed.), *Aggressive behavior: Current perspectives* (pp. 97–130). New York: Plenum.

Olweus, D. (1995a). Bullying or peer abuse at school: Facts and interventions. *Current Directions in Psychological Science, 4*(6), 196–200.

Olweus, D. (1995b). Bullying or peer abuse at school: Intervention and prevention. In G. Davies & S. Lloyd-Bostock (Eds.), *Psychology, law, and criminal justice: International developments in research and practice.* Oxford, UK: Walter De Gruyter.

Olweus, D., Limber, S., & Mihalic, S. (1999). *Blueprints for violence prevention: The Bullying Prevention Program.* Boulder, CO: Center for the Study and Prevention of Violence.

Orpinas, P., & Horne, A. M. (2006). *Bullying prevention: Creating a positive school climate and developing social competence.* Washington, DC: American Psychological Association.

Ozer, E. J., Tschann, J. M., Pasch, L. A., & Flores, E. (2004). Violence perpetration across peer and partner relationships: Co-occurrences and longitudinal patterns among adolescents. *Journal of Adolescent Health, 34,* 64–71.

Patchin, J. W., & Hinduja, S. (2006). Bullies move beyond the schoolyard: A preliminary look at cyberbullying. *Youth Violence and Juvenile Justice, 4,* 148–169.

Pellegrini, A. D. (2001). A longitudinal study of heterosexual relationships, aggression, and sexual harassment during the transition from primary school through middle school. *Applied Developmental Psychology, 22,* 119–133.

Pellegrini, A. D. (2002a). Affiliative and aggressive dimensions of dominance and possible functions during early adolescence. *Aggression and Violent Behavior, 7,* 21–31.

Pellegrini, A. D. (2002b). Bullying, victimization, and sexual harassment during the transition to middle school. *Educational Psychologist, 37,* 151–163.

Pellegrini, A. D., & Bartini, M. (2001). Dominance in early adolescent boys: Affiliative and aggressive dimensions and possible functions. *Merrill-Palmer Quarterly, 47,* 142–163.

Pellegrini, A. D., & Long, J. (2002). A longitudinal study of bullying, dominance, and victimization during the transition from primary to secondary school. *British Journal of Developmental Psychology, 20,* 259–280.

Pepler, D. J., Craig, W. M., Connolly, J., & Henderson, K. (2002). Bullying, sexual harassment, dating violence, and substance use among adolescents. In C. Wekerle & A.-M. Wall (Eds.), *The violence and addiction equation: Theoretical and clinical issues in substance abuse and relationship violence* (pp. 153–168). New York: Brunner-Routledge.

Pepler, D. J., Craig, W. M., Connolly, J. A., Yuile, A., McMaster, L., & Jiang, D. (2006). A developmental perspective on bullying. *Aggressive Behavior, 32,* 376–384.

Pepler, D., Craig, W., & O'Connell, P. (in press). Peer processes in bullying: Informing prevention and intervention strategies. In S. R. Jimerson, S. M. Swearer, & D. L. Espelage (Eds.), *The international handbook of school bullying.* New York: Routledge.

Pesznecker, K. (2004, July 1). District settled suit for millions. *Anchorage Daily News.*

Pew Internet. (2005a, July 25). Teens forge forward with the Internet and other new technologies. Retrieved October 23, 2007, from *www.pewinternet.org/press_release.asp?r=109.*

Pew Internet. (2005b, July 27). Teens and technology: Youth are leading the transition to a fully wired and mobile nation. Retrieved October 23, 2007, from *www.pewinternet.org/ppf/r/162/report_display.asp.*

Pew Internet & American Life Project. (2008, February 15). Demographics of Internet users. In October 24–December 2, 2007, from tracking survey. Retrieved June 9, 2008, from *www.pewinternet.org/trends/User_Demo_2.15.08.htm.*

Pollack, W. (1998). *Real boys: Rescuing our sons from the myths of boyhood.* New York: Henry Holt.

Ray v. Antioch Unified School District, 107 F. Supp. 2d 1165 (N.D. Cal. 2000).

Rehabilitation Act of 1973, 29 U.S.C. § 794 (2006) ("Section 504 of the Rehabilitation Act").

Respect for All Project. (2004). *Let's get real: Curriculum guide.* San Francisco: Women's Educational Media.

Reynolds, C. R., & Kamphaus, R. W. (2004). *Behavior Assessment System for Children manual* (2nd ed.). Bloomington, MN: Pearson Assessments.

Reynolds, W. M. (2003). *Reynolds Bully-Victimization Scales for Schools.* San Antonio, TX: Psychological Corporation.

Rhode Island Department of Education. (n.d.). Guidance on developing required policies against bullying. Retrieved April 1, 2008, from *www.ride.ri.gov/psi/DOCS/20030102_GuidancePolicyBullying.*

Rigby, K., & Slee, P. (1993). Dimensions of interpersonal relation among Australian children and implications for psychological well-being. *Journal of School Psychology, 133*, 33–42.

Rodkin, R. C., Farmer, T. W., Pearl, R., & Van Acker, R. (2000). Heterogeneity of popular boys: Antisocial and prosocial configurations. *Developmental Psychology, 36*, 14–24.

Rodkin, R. C., Farmer, T. W., Pearl, R., & Van Acker, R. (2006). They're cool: Social status and peer group supports for aggressive boys and girls. *Social Development, 15*, 175–204.

Rodkin, P. C., & Hodges, E. V. (2003). Bullies and victims in the peer ecology: Four questions for psychologists and school professionals. *School Psychology Review, 32*(3), 384–400.

Rodkin, P. C., & Wilson, T. (2007). Aggression and adaptation: Psychological record, educational promise. In P. H. Hawley, T. D. Little, & P. C. Rodkin (Eds.), *Aggression and adaptation: The bright side to bad behavior* (pp. 235–267). Mahwah, NJ: Erlbaum.

Rutter, M., Maughan, B., Mortimore, P., Ouston, J., & Smith, A. (1979). *Fifteen thousand hours: Secondary schools and their effects on children.* Cambridge, MA: Harvard University Press.

Salmivalli, C., Lagerspetz, K., Bjorkqvist, K., Osterman, K., & Kaukiainen, A. (1996). Bullying as a group process: Participant roles and their relations to social status within group. *Aggressive Behavior, 22*, 1–15.

School Bullying Prevention Act, Oklahoma Statute 70, § 24-100.3 (2005).

Schwartz, D., Dodge, K. A., Pettit, G. S., & Bates, J. E. (1997). The early socialization of aggressive victims of bullying. *Child Development, 68*, 665–675.

Schwartz, D., Gorman, A. H., Nakamoto, J., & Toblin, R. L. (2005). Victimization in the peer group and children's academic functioning. *Journal of Educational Psychology, 97*, 425–435.

Seals, D., & Young, J. (2003). Bullying and victimization: Prevalence and relationship to gender, grade level, ethnicity, self-esteem, and depression. *Adolescence, 38*(152), 735–747.

Seper, C. (2005, February 14). School bullies can land in court. *The Plain Dealer.*

Sheridan, S. M., Napolitano, S. A., & Swearer, S. M. (2002). Best practices in school-community partnerships. In A. Thomas & J. Grimes (Eds.), *Best practices in school psychology* (4th ed., pp. 322–336). Bethesda, MD: National Association of School Psychologists.

Shields, A., & Cicchetti, D. (2001). Parental maltreatment and emotion dysregulation as risk factors for bullying and victimization in middle childhood. *Journal of Clinical Child Psychology, 30*, 349–363.

Skiba, R. J., & Knesting, K. (2002). Zero tolerance, zero evidence: An analysis of school disciplinary practice. In R. J. Skiba & G. G. Noam (Eds.), *New directions for youth development: No 92. Zero tolerance: Can suspension and expulsion keep schools safe?* (pp. 17–43). San Francisco: Jossey-Bass.

Skiba, R., Reynolds, C. R., Graham, S., Sheras, P., Conoley, J. C., & Garcia-Vazquez, E. (2006, February). Are zero tolerance policies effective in the schools?: An evidentiary review and recommendations. Retrieved March 19, 2007, from *www.apa.org/releases/ZTTFReportBPDRevisions5-15.pdf.*

Smith, J. D., Schneider, B. H., Smith, P. K., & Ananiadou, K. (2004). The effectiveness of whole-school antibullying programs: A synthesis of evaluation research. *School Psychology Review, 33*, 547–560.

Smith, P. K. (2007). Why has aggression been thought of as maladaptive? In P. H. Hawley, T. D. Little, & P. C. Rodkin (Eds.), *Aggression and adaptation: The bright side to bad behavior* (pp. 65–83). Mahwah, NJ: Erlbaum.

Smith, P. K., Bowers, L., Binney, V., & Cowie, H. (1993). Relationships of children involved in bully/victim problems at school. In S. Duck (Ed.), *Learning about relationships* (pp. 184–212). London: Sage.

Smith, P. K., Cowie, H., Olafsson, R. F., Liefooghe, A. P., Almeida, A., & Araki, H., et al. (2002). Definitions of bullying: A comparison of terms used, and age and gender differences in a fourteen-country international comparison. *Child Development, 73*, 1119–1133.

Smith, P. K., Morita, Y., Junger-Tas, J., Olweus, D., Catalano, R. F., & Slee, P. (1999). *The nature of school bullying: A cross-national perspective.* Florence, KY: Taylor & Frances/Routledge.

Smith, P. K., & Myron-Wilson, R. (1998). Parenting and school bullying. *Child Psychology and Psychiatry, 3*, 405–417.

Snelling v. Fall Mountain Regional School District, 2001 DNH 57 (D.N.H. 2001).

Solberg, M. E., Olweus, D., & Endresen, I. M. (2007). Bullies and victims at school: Are they the same pupils? *British Journal of Educational Psychology, 77*, 441–464.

Soutter, A., & McKenzie, A. (2000). The use and effects of anti-bullying and anti-harassment policies in Australian schools. *School Psychology International, 21*, 96–105.

Sprague, J. R., & Walker, H. M. (2005). *Safe and healthy schools: Practical prevention strategies.* New York: Guilford Press

Srabstein, J. C., McCarter, R. J., Shao, C., & Huang, Z. J. (2006). Morbidities associated with bullying behaviors in adolescents: School based study of American adolescents. *International Journal of Adolescent Medicine and Health, 18*, 587–596.

State of New Jersey, Department of Education. (2007). Model policy and guidance for prohibiting harassment, intimidation and bullying on school property, at school-sponsored functions and on school buses. Retrieved April 1, 2008, from *www.state.nj.us/education/parents/bully.pdf*.

Stevens, V., De Bourdeaudhuji, I., & Van Oost, P. (2002). Relationship of the family environment to children's involvement in bully/victim problems at school. *Journal of Youth and Adolescence, 31*, 419–428.

Stevenson v. Martin County Board of Education, 3 Fed. Appx. 25 (4th Cir. 2001).

Stop Bullying Now. (n.d.). All about bullying. Retrieved September 12, 2006, from *www.stopbullyingnow.hrsa.gov/adult/indexAdult.asp?Area=allaboutbullying*.

Strom, P. S., & Strom, R. D. (2005). Cyberbullying by adolescents: A preliminary assessment. *The Educational Forum, 70*, 21–23.

Sutton, J., Smith, P. K., & Swettenham, J. (1999). Bullying and "theory of mind": A critique of the "social skills deficit" view of anti-social behaviour. *Social Development 8*, 117–127.

Swearer, S. M., Cary, P. T., & Frazier-Koontz, M. (2001, August). *Attitudes toward bullying in middle school youth: A developmental examination across the bully/victim continuum.* Paper presented at the 109th Annual Convention of the American Psychological Association, San Francisco, CA.

Swearer, S. M., & Doll, B. (2001). Bullying in schools: An ecological framework. *Journal of Emotional Abuse, 2*, 7–23.

Swearer, S. M., & Espelage, D. L. (2004). Introduction: A social-ecological framework of bullying among youth. In D. L. Espelage & S. M. Swearer (Eds.), *Bullying in American schools: A social-ecological perspective on prevention and intervention* (pp. 1–12). Mahwah, NJ: Erlbaum.

Swearer, S. M., & Givens, J. E. (March, 2006). *Designing an alternative to suspension for middle school bullies.* Paper presented at the annual convention of the National Association of School Psychologists, Anaheim, CA.

Swearer, S. M., Peugh, J., Espelage, D. L., Siebecker, A. B., Kingsbury, W., & Bevins, K. S. (2006). A socioecological model for bullying prevention and intervention in early adolescence: An exploratory examination. In S. R. Jimerson & M. J. Furlong (Eds.), *Handbook of school violence and school safety: From research to practice* (pp. 257–273). Mahwah, NJ: Erlbaum.

Swearer, S. M., Song, S. Y., Cary, P. T., Eagle, J. W., & Mickelson, W. T. (2001). Psychosocial correlates in bullying and victimization: The relationship between depression, anxiety, and bully/victim status. *Journal of Emotional Abuse, 2,* 95–121.

Tennessee Code Annotated § 49-6-1016 (2005).

Theno v. Tonganoxie Unified School District No. 464, 394 F. Supp. 2d 1299 (D. Kan. 2005).

Troy, M., & Sroufe, L. A. (1987). Victimization among preschoolers: Role of attachment relationship history. *Journal of the American Academy of Child and Adolescent Psychiatry, 26,* 166–172.

Tynes, B., Reynolds, L., & Greenfield, P. M. (2004). Adolescence, race, and ethnicity on the Internet: A comparison of discourse in monitored vs. unmonitored chat rooms. *Applied Developmental Psychology, 25,* 667–684.

Underwood, M. K. (2003). *Social aggression among girls.* New York: Guilford Press.

Unnever, J. (2005). Bullies, aggressive victims and victims: Are they distinct groups? *Aggressive Behavior, 31,* 153–171.

U.S. Census Bureau News. (2005, October 27). Computer and Internet use in the United States: 2003. Retrieved October 23, 2007, from *www.census.gov/Press-Release/www/releases/archives/miscellaneous/005863.html.*

Vaillancourt, T., Hymel, S., & McDougall, P. (2003). Bullying is power: Implications for school-based intervention strategies. *Journal of Applied School Psychology, 19,* 157–176.

VandenBos, G. R. (2007). *APA dictionary of psychology.* Washington, DC: American Psychological Association.

Vermont Department of Education. (n.d.). Model bullying prevention plan. Retrieved from *education.vermont.gov/new/pdfdoc/pgm_safeschools/pubs/bullying_prevention_04.pdf.*

Vossekuil, B., Fein, R. A., Reddy, M., Borum, R., & Modzeleski, W. (2002). *The final report and findings of the safe school initiative: Implications for the prevention of school attacks in the United States.* Washington, DC: U.S. Secret Services and U.S. Department of Education.

Vreeman, R. C., & Carroll, A. E. (2007). A systematic review of school-based interventions to prevent bullying. *Archives of Pediatric Adolescent Medicine, 161,* 78–88.

Washington Virginia Code Annotated § 18-2C-4 (Michie 2006a).

Washington Virginia Code Annotated § 18-2C-5 (Michie 2006b).

Washington Revised Code § 28A.300.285 (2006).

Washington State School Safety Center. (2002). Prohibition of harassment, intimidation and bullying. Retrieved April 1, 2008, from *www.k12.wa.us/SafetyCenter/pubdocs/ModelPolicy.doc.*

Washington v. Pierce, 2005 VT 125 (VT 2005).

Washingtonpost.com. (2005, July 7). Connecting with kids, wirelessly. Retrieved June 9, 2008, from *www.washingtonpost.com/wp-dyn/content/article/2005/07/06/AR2005070602100.html.*

Wentzel, K. R., & Caldwell, K. A. (1997). Friendships, peer acceptance, and group membership: Relations to academic achievement in middle school. *Child Development, 68,* 1198–1209.

Wenxin, Z. (2002). Prevalence and major characteristics of bullying/victimization among primary and junior middle school students. *Acta Psychologica Sinica, 34,* 387–394.

WIBW.com. (2005, December 24). School bullying. Retrieved December 9, 2006, from *www.wibw.com/home/headlines/2115597.html.*

Willard, N. E. (2004). An educator's guide to cyberbullying and cyberthreats. Retrieved June 9, 2008, from *cyberbully.org/cyberbully/docs/cbcteducator.pdf.*

Willard, N. E. (2007). *Cyberbullying and cyberthreats: Responding to the challenge of online social aggression, threats, and distress.* Champaign, IL: Research Press.

Ybarra, M. L. (2004). Linkages between depressive symtomatology and Internet harassment among young regular Internet users. *CyberPsychology and Behavior, 7,* 247–257.

Ybarra, M. L., Espelage, D. L., & Mitchell, K. (2007). The co-occurrence of Internet harassment and unwanted sexual solicitation victimization and perpetration: Associations with psychosocial indicators. *Journal of Adolescent Health, 41,* S31–S41.

Ybarra, M. L., & Mitchell, K. J. (2004a). Online aggresssors/targets, aggressors, and targets: A comparison of associated youth characteristics. *Journal of Child Psychology and Psychiatry, 45,* 1308–1316.

Ybarra, M. L., & Mitchell, K. J. (2004b). Youth engaging in online harassment: Associations with caregiver–child relationships, Internet use, and personal characteristics. *Journal of Adolescence, 27,* 319–336.

Ybarra, M. L., Mitchell, K. J., Wolak, J., & Finkelhor, D. (2006). Examining characteristics and associated distress related to Internet harassment: Findings from the Second Youth Internet Safety Survey. *Pediatrics, 118,* e1169–e1177.

Ybarra, M. L., & Suman, M. (2006). Help seeking behavior and the Internet: A national survey. *International Journal of Medical Informatics, 75,* 29–41.

Author Index

Subject Index